Random Kinds of
FACTNESS

Random Kinds of
FACTNESS

1001

(or So)

Absolutely True Tidbits
About (Mostly) Everything

ERIN BARRETT AND JACK MINGO

CONARI PRESS

First published in 2005 by Conari Press,
an imprint of Red Wheel/Weiser, LLC
York Beach, ME
With offices at:
368 Congress Street
Boston, MA 02210
www.redwheelweiser.com

Library of Congress Cataloging-in-Publication Data

Barrett, Erin.
Random kinds of factness : 1001 (or so) absolutely true tidbits about
(mostly) everything / Erin Barrett and Jack Mingo.
p. cm.
ISBN 1-57324-212-8 (alk. paper)
1. Curiosities and wonders. I. Title: 1001 (or so) absolutely true
tidbits about (mostly) everything. II. Mingo, Jack. III. Title.
AG243.B33 2005
031.02—dc22
2005015502

Typeset in Bulmer by Lisa Buckley Design
Printed in the United States of America
VG

12 11 10 09 08 07 06 05
8 7 6 5 4 3 2 1

CONTENTS

You probably already know that reading fun facts can be like eating peanuts (which are neither a pea nor a nut, but a legume). It's hard to stop once you start. You may not know, though, that writing fun facts is likewise addicting. So addicting, that it's hard to stop. In fact, after we started writing them, we eventually found ourselves writing everything—novels, love letters, even introductions to books—in the fun-fact style.

We have been writing a daily newspaper column called Random Kinds of Factness for three years now. We know so many components of so many things that we wonder sometimes if we really know anything at all.

Some experts claim that we have more fun facts than any other time of history. However, others argue that the total number of fun facts remains constant year after year.

We know that some fun facts disappear every year. This ever-disappearing nature of individual fun facts is a reason to buy this book and cherish its contents. People like reading fun facts because it makes them feel smart.

Unless you're writing a column or a book, sharing fun facts is not a good way to find companionship at social gatherings. Despite all reasonable expectations, you will not be considered the life of the party, and will likely find yourself alone in a corner, drinking heavily.

People who like reading fun facts are the same people who like that disorienting feeling that comes when their paradigm shifts slightly to the left.

If you learn a lot of fun facts, people no longer invite you to play trivia games. That's partly because you play it so well, but it's also partly because they'll become annoyed when you nitpick the game's facts.

But knowing a lot of fun facts *can* make you feel smugly superior. Jump into this book and enjoy!

Erin Barrett and Jack Mingo

AMERICANA

Before it was painted white in 1814, the White House was called "the Presidential Palace."

In the 1950s, nearly 50 percent of American workers were unionized. It was a time of unprecedented gains in wages and benefits. Today, only 15 percent of American workers belong to unions.

Circus fans, do you know how many Ringling Brothers there were? Seven. Al, Gus, Otto, Alf, Charles, John, and Henry. They had a sister, too, named Ida.

How many children did George Washington have? Although he was "Father of His Country," Washington had no biological children of his own.

If you're an average American, you'll spend about a year and a half of your life watching TV commercials.

It's not just a popular stereotype; most barns in the 1800s really were painted red. Why was that? Red paint hid dirt well and was easy to make without having to resort to expensive store-bought paint. Here's the recipe: Mix skim milk with some linseed oil and lime. Add rust that you scraped off some old farm tools for the pigment. Voilà!

President John Quincy Adams kept a pet alligator around the White House. He said he enjoyed "the spectacle of guests fleeing from the room in terror."

In Maine, log cabins are exempt from property taxes.

In 1920, the average bill at an everyday diner was 28 cents.

"Kiki" was the childhood nickname of Supreme Court Justice Ruth Bader Ginsberg.

So far, all U.S. presidents have had siblings. Not one has been an only child.

U.S. founding father, George Washington, was a leader in more ways than the obvious. He was first to introduce the mule to America, and he is also considered the Father of the American Foxhound.

The very first American entrepreneur to be worth a billion dollars? Car mogul Henry Ford.

It may be hard to imagine a time when presidents took pride in cultural pursuits, but two presidents actually published books of poetry: John Quincy Adams and Jimmy Carter.

What do you call a president? George Washington wanted to be called "His Mightiness, the President." John Adams preferred "His Highness, the President of the United States and Protector of their Liberties." Neither title caught on. Finally, democratic Thomas Jefferson came up with "Mr. President."

Thomas Jefferson was also the first president to actually shake hands with people. Previous presidents preferred a slight, dignified bow and no body contact.

In the 1880s, about 15 percent of all city dwellers in America had access to an indoor bathroom.

John Breckinridge at thirty-six was the youngest vice president, followed by Richard Nixon, thirty-nine.

Larger than life: The Statue of Liberty is about twenty times bigger than an average American woman. From her toes to the top of her head, she measures a bit over 111 feet.

The term "french fries" was coined by our favorite president Thomas Jefferson. He brought back samples of the fried potato sticks from France and dubbed them "Potatoes fried in the French manner." Americans are an efficient lot, so shortened the name to "french fries."

In the United States, more gold is used to make class rings than any other piece of jewelry.

Benjamin Franklin was the father of the bifocals, the stove, and the Constitution, but did you also know that he was controversial in his time as an advocate of taking baths? Puritans had made bathing illegal on the grounds that nudity of any kind—even in the privacy of your own bath—was a sin. Ben argued that the laws should be repealed. They were, eventually.

Was the Statue of Liberty modeled after a specific person? Two people to be exact. Sculptor Frédéric-Auguste Bartholdi used his mother as the model for Liberty's face and his girlfriend as the model for her body. Dr. Freud will see you now, Monsieur Bartholdi.

There's only one crime mentioned by name in the entire U.S. Constitution: treason.

How much does it actually cost to mint our coins? A penny costs about half a cent; a nickel, 2.5 cents; a dime, 1 cent; a quarter 3 cents; and a half-dollar, 5 cents.

Hey, it's tax deductible: every year, American citizens donate about $1 million to the United States government to reduce the national debt.

It is a criminal offense for a sailor or soldier to pose nude, under the U.S. Uniform Code of Military Justice.

There've been quite a few Jims in the White House over the years. As a matter of fact, James is the most popular presidential first name—there have been six so far. John and William tie for the second most popular president's name.

We have it on good authority that there are 132 rooms in the White House. Thirty-two of them are bathrooms.

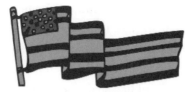

During the Cold War, the U.S. Federal Emergency Management Agency advised that each of the following can block radiation as well as 4 inches of concrete: 18 inches of wood; 5–6 inches of brick; 8 inches of hollow concrete block; 7 inches of soil; 6 inches of sand; 10 inches of water; or 14 inches of books or magazines.

If you vote by absentee ballot but die before election day, what happens? Your vote still counts.

Only one-third of American presidents have not been lawyers.

The smallest U. S. president was James Madison, measuring 5 feet 4 inches and weighing in at 98 pounds.

Hubert H. Humphrey kept his pharmacy license as a backup in case his thirty-one-year political career didn't pan out.

F. Scott Fitzgerald's full name was Francis Scott Key Fitzgerald. He was second cousin, three times removed, of the man who wrote the U.S. national anthem.

 Most people assume that stamping on U. S. currency "In God We Trust" has a long tradition. Actually, it was mandated in 1955. During those jittery Cold War days, Congress also added "under God" to the Pledge of Allegiance, and "so help me God" to the official oath of office.

On a sad November day in 1963, Lyndon Baines Johnson had to phone three Dallas lawyers before he found one who had a copy of the presidential oath of office. He needed it so that he could be sworn in on Air Force One after President Kennedy was killed.

Worried about natural disasters? Add all the Americans who die in an average year from tornadoes, earthquakes, and floods, and you'll get a total of less than two hundred. Contrast that with the number of city dwellers who die from summer heat in a typical year: about fifteen hundred.

How do you get into the Fort Knox gold repository? Not easily. Only after several trusted individuals dial their own secret combinations can the 20-ton door creak slowly open.

Believe it or not, the presidential oath of office that each incoming president must recite is only thirty-five words long. You'd think there'd be more.

Before coming to his *Common Sense*, revolutionary writer Thomas Paine was a corset maker and tax collector.

Just minutes after being injured in an assassination attempt, Teddy Roosevelt calmly carried on with a speech in Milwaukee. Afterward, doctors removed the bullet that had lodged in his chest.

Thomas Jefferson authored the Declaration of Independence at age thirty-three.

Who said obsessive dictionary authors don't have a sense of humor? Noah Webster suggested, tongue firmly planted in cheek, that the following articles also be added to the Bill of Rights: guaranteed good weather and fishing, no restraints on sensible eating or drinking, and when tired of lying on your right side, the guaranteed right to lie on your left side or your back.

Annie Taylor, a school teacher from Bay City, Michigan, became the first person to go over Niagara Falls in a barrel. The year was 1901. Her advice: "No one ought ever do that again."

Richard Nixon had always wanted to work for the FBI. So much so that he applied before he'd graduated from law school. He wasn't accepted. In fact, he never even received a reply, so he went down a different path and became president instead.

The worst battle for American soldiers was the Civil War. Between bullets and disease, the average Johnny had a one in six chance of not marching home again.

The song "Yankee Doodle" began as a nonsense Dutch song called "Yankee Dudel Doodle Down" in the fifteenth century. It spread to England as a children's song before being used to taunt Oliver Cromwell's Protestants during the English Civil War.

Finally, the Brits turned it on the American colonists in the same taunting vein, not realizing that we'd adopt it proudly.

The man who invented condensed milk also coined the rallying cry, "Remember the Alamo!" That was Gail Borden, who was a newspaper editor before he founded the milk products company that bears his name.

The Capitol Building in Washington, D.C., has 365 steps—one for every day of most years—no more, no less. If you were born on February 29 in a leap year, you're out of luck.

In a "Who Has the Biggest Face?" face-off, the boys on Mount Rushmore come in first with faces about 60 feet tall. The Sphinx in Egypt comes in second with a 30-foot mug. In comparison, the Statue of Liberty is a l'il lady, with only about 20 feet from chin to forehead. In case you're thinking of buying her some gloves, the index finger of the Statue of Liberty is 8 feet long.

Giving credit where it's due, Paul Revere was one of the participants at the Boston Tea Party. However, he didn't make the ride he's most famous for. That was an invention by poet Henry Wadsworth Longfellow. In reality, Revere was turned back by the Redcoats—it was Dr. Samuel Prescott who rode to Concord shouting, "The British are coming!"

President Grover Cleveland, weighing in at 280 pounds, was nicknamed "Big Steve" and "Uncle Jumbo."

On July 13, 1985, George H. W. Bush became the first vice president to serve as acting president. He held the position for eight hours while Ronald Reagan underwent surgery to remove a colon tumor.

Undereducated presidents are not a new phenomenon. Andrew Jackson, Andrew Johnson, and Zachary Taylor never even graduated from elementary school.

July 4, 1826, was a big day in American history. It was the Declaration of Independence's fiftieth anniversary, Thomas Jefferson and John Adams both died, and Stephen Foster's mom gave birth to the Americana-besotted songwriter.

Other Fourth of July presidential milestones: James Monroe died July 4, 1831, exactly five years after Adams and Jefferson. President Zachary Taylor celebrated a hot July 4, 1850, with speeches and too much picnic food, then took to his  bed with acute indigestion and died five days later. And Calvin Coolidge was born on July 4, 1872.

"Yankee Doodle Dandy" songwriter George M. Cohan claimed that he was born on the Fourth of July, 1878. It's a good story, but his baptismal record says his birth took place on July 3.

You know there's a crack in the Liberty Bell, but do you know when it happened? On July 8, 1835, while being rung during the funeral of John Marshall, chief justice of the United States.

The Constitution says that presidents must be native-born citizens, yet eight of ours weren't born in the United States. How can this be? Easy—the first eight presidents were born before the United States was founded, in what were then England's American colonies.

Richard Stockton, one of the signers of the Declaration of Independence, had a change of heart during the war and signed an oath of loyalty to the king. However, later, as the revolutionaries gained ground, Stockton switched sides once again. Smart man.

Explain this one, if you can: all American presidents with facial hair also happened to be Republicans.

Five presidents had beards; four had mustaches but no beard. Of the five who had beards, two were assassinated.

ANIMALS

Besides humans, the Asian elephant is the only animal we know of that can stand on its head.

Although humans have bred this out of the farm version, turkeys in the wild can run at speeds of up to 20 mph, and fly at about 55 mph.

American cats have it good: 67 percent of them are allowed to sleep in the bed with their owners.

The biggest hog ever recorded was Big Bill from Jackson, Tennessee. He weighed a whopping 2,552 pounds, and was about 9 feet in length.

Why are bulldogs called that? The breed was originally bred for bullbaiting—to tear apart chained bulls for the amusement of spectators in jolly olde England. Dog breeders have since bred the viciousness out of the breed, and they now make good pets.

After penguin moms lay their eggs, penguin dads are left to incubate them for weeks afterward. Emperor penguin dads do this by balancing the eggs on the topsides of their feet with their ample bellies hanging over them, twenty-four hours a day for weeks.

In America, you have about a one in 3,448,276 chance of dying from a snakebite.

You may already know that a group of frogs is called a "chorus." Did you know, though, a group of toads is called a "knot"?

Cue the hysterical laughter of cat owners everywhere: health care professionals in medieval times thought that owning a cat would cure insanity.

Remember Felix the Cat? The cartoon character's name was a pun on the Latin term for the house cat, *Felis catus.*

Thailand (Siam) doesn't take credit for the Siamese cat. The people there call it "the Chinese cat."

Got an alligator clamped around your arm? Try poking its eye or punching its nose. We've heard these are the best ways to get free of its grip . . . however, we guarantee nothing.

Farmers say that pigs love eating rattlers, gobbling the poisonous snakes up before they have a chance to strike.

If you're an ailurophobe (cat hater), you can blame the Pilgrims for likely bringing the first domestic cats to the New World.

Cows, sheep, dogs, and goats are aplenty in the Bible, but cats are never even mentioned once.

Lizards and flies never lose their suction when climbing on walls, because they don't use suction. Microscopic grooves on their feet grab microscopic pits and scratches, even on a "smooth" surface like glass.

You're probably not going to see a horror movie about it, but more people are killed by pigs than sharks every year.

Why are those wrinkled Chinese dogs called "shar-pei"? It's a Chinese word meaning "sharkskin."

Baby alligators signal to their mothers that they're ready to emerge from their eggs. They have to, because she has to dig them out of the mud before they can hatch. What's the signal? A loud barking that can be heard from 50 feet away.

You might not think it, but an alligator mom is a great parent. Unlike many reptiles, she stays with her young for two years, protecting them from predators by letting them ride on her back or in her mouth.

It may be a big animal, but an alligator's brain is only about as big as your thumb. What's pitiful is that, small as an alligator's brain is, the alligator has one of the largest reptilian brains in proportion to its size.

If kept safe from foxes, frying pans, and Colonel Sanders, chickens can live about eight years.

How many lives have the legendary St. Bernards of the Alps saved? The big sloppy rescue dogs with a brandy cask are credited with rescuing twenty-five hundred people over the last two hundred years.

A cow consumes the equivalent of a bathtub full of water every day. Granted some of the moisture comes from the grass it eats, but it all adds up to about 50 gallons.

Bovines are cattle, but what are ovines? Sheep.

Yes, you can train a zebra to pull a horse wagon.

These names will live in history: Doreena Cary, Diane Greib, Kathy Roads, and Dorothy McCarthy. On October 9, 1976, they set the chicken-plucking world record by defeathering twelve birds in less than thirty-three seconds.

Where did Jack Russell terriers get their name? From the man who first bred them in the 1800s, the Reverend John ("Jack") Russell.

The largest frog in the world is about the size of your average pet cat. It's the aptly named goliath frog from West Africa.

In contrast, the Brazilian gold frog is only about an eighth of an inch long.

A reader asks how many neck bones a giraffe has? The answer is seven, same as people and almost every other mammal. They are extra-long, though.

Male marsupials of all kinds have a forked penis. What purpose might this serve, you may well ask? Well, female marsupials all have two uteruses that branch off from a forked opening. You know what they say: There's someone for everybody.

Those inventors at the Dubai Camel Hospital are pretty ingenious. The operating table has a big hole cut in the middle of it. That's for camel humps. The table is lowered on top of a sitting camel, the camel is strapped in, and the table is mechanically moved upright so the animal is belly-up, with all four legs in the air, and ready for surgery.

Hair apparent: Your average cat usually has twelve whiskers on each side of its face.

An ostrich egg measures about 5 inches wide and 4 inches tall. It's big enough to make eleven omelets—a feat that normally requires twenty chicken eggs.

Even though they may happen to have an orange glow, the name orangutan actually comes from the Malay language and means "person of the forest."

Cheetahs are fast, reaching speeds of about 71 mph.

Kangaroos? Don't sell them short. They can reach speeds of up to 40 mph, hopping 33 feet at a time.

A beaver can swim more than half a mile underwater on one single breath of air.

Cats can drive even a genius crazy, what with that out-again, in-again thing they do. Sir Isaac Newton's cat Spithead kept interrupting his work on the laws of gravity, so he put his intellect to work. He invented that sanity-saving contraption, the cat-door flap.

The male right whale's testicles weigh more than a ton, accounting for about 1 percent of its body weight.

It wasn't until 1841, twenty years after a major fossil find in England, that Western-world scientists began to piece together the dinosaur puzzle. Before that date, any large bones found were presumed to belong to giant humans, wiped out in the Biblical flood.

The white rhino isn't white, but gray. It was originally called *weit* (wide) by the Dutch. They were describing the *weit* rhino's snouts, perfectly suited for eating grass.

Although protective parents fret about such things, the truth is that there has never been a documented case of a squirrel passing rabies on to a human.

An elephant's ears can be up to 6.5 feet long and just as wide.

In the 1930s, it wasn't a baseball or football star, but a wild-animal trainer named Maria Rasputin who first appeared on a box of Wheaties.

Odd animal, the duck-billed platypus. Its leathery bill is highly sensitive, the better to guide it through murky water. It's a mammal, but lays eggs. The female's milk comes not from nipples, but from pores on its chest and sides, and the babies then lick it off her fur.

The average adult giraffe tongue measures just less than 2 feet in length.

No one knows for sure where the penguin got its name. Many speculate logically that the name came from the Welsh words *pen*, meaning "head," and *gwyn*, meaning "white."

The crab-eater seal eats krill, not crabs.

According to (human) scientists, here's the Top Ten list of the most intelligent animals on earth: humans, chimpanzees, gorillas, orangutans, baboons, gibbons, monkeys, small-toothed whales such as the killer whale, dolphins, elephants.

In general a penguin can have up to seventy feathers per square inch on its body. There's a good reason for the density: feathers are wonderful insulation. You can go ahead and add penguins to the list of animals that mate for life. Unfortunately for them, it doesn't pay off that well—they still only have sex once a year.

Cats have thirty-two muscles around their ears, allowing them to turn each ear independently.

If you've got a short-haired house cat, its ancestors were bred in ancient Egypt from an African wildcat (*Felis libyca*). If you've got a long-haired cat, its ancestors were bred in ancient India from an Asian wildcat (*Felix manul*).

Chickens can fly. They're much better than an ostrich, emu, penguin, or a kiwi. That's not saying much, though. The world-record flight of a chicken is only about 230 yards.

Flamingos have been around a long time. Virtually unchanged over time, the species has roamed Earth for about forty-seven million years.

When a cat half closes its eyes while looking at you, it's a sign of trust. Do it back to them, and you'll have a bonding experience.

Yes, dogs have bellybuttons. They're little slits hidden by fur.

Hippos are closely related to pigs.

Female lions may be vicious to other animals, but a lion cub can go to any nursing female in its pride and be assured of milk.

Want to get a hippo to open its mouth and say "ah"? Tickle its nose.

Armadillos accidentally eat a lot of dirt with their diets of small insects and snails, which is why their excrement looks like piles of clay marbles.

Newborn baby giraffes are more than 5 feet tall. Good thing, too—they drop about 6 feet to the ground during the birth process.

Most Americans mispronounce "armadillo." It's a Spanish word, so you should say it "arm-a-dee-yo." What's it mean, you ask? "Little man in armor."

A reader asks if any wild monkeys ever lived in Europe. Actually, they still do. Barbary apes live on the Rock of Gibraltar on the tip of Spain.

Gorillas' arms are longer than their legs. Measure a typical male gorilla and you'll find that its arm span is about 8 feet.

 A baby chick inside its egg breathes through more than eight thousand pores in its eggshell.

You know the mountain gorillas that were featured in the movie *Gorillas in the Mist*? There are fewer than 650 left in the wild today.

Alligator or crocodile? Not that it matters much if one is chasing you. Alligators have a broad, square snout. Crocodiles have a more narrow snout, and their bottom teeth stick out when their mouths are shut.

It's only the cheetah that runs down its prey. Most other cats use the stalk-and-pounce method.

Most hippos live in herds, but the little pygmy hippo is a solitary creature.

Brine shrimp (known by kids as "sea monkeys") can live in water that's about six times saltier than regular seawater.

Goats have tough lips they use like fingertips to explore new things. This has given them the erroneous reputation of being a walking garbage can. They're actually pretty particular about what they eat.

We wonder if the Audubon Society knew about this when they chose their name? John James Audubon made his paintings of birds look so realistic by using freshly killed specimens and wiring them into naturalistic poses. He claimed that dead birds lost their color quickly, so he shot as many as a hundred a day for his art.

First First Lady Martha Washington owned a parrot that George couldn't stand. The parrot likewise hated George. Whenever they were in the same room, they watched each other like hawks for any false moves.

Biologists tell us that bats always turn left when they exit a cave.

What lurks below? There are jellyfish in every ocean in the world. On top of that, there are even freshwater jellyfish that can live in lakes.

Sharks can hear notes lower than humans can hear; however, humans can hear notes higher than sharks can.

Are you safe from sharks if you're in a freshwater river? Not necessarily. The bull shark (*Carcharhinus leucas*) frequently swims far up rivers from the ocean.

On the other hand, shark attacks are extremely rare: fewer than one hundred a year worldwide, with only twenty-five to thirty fatalities. Given the number of people who visit the beach, you're more likely to die in the auto taking you there.

No, it's not true that camels store water in their humps. The humps are filled with fat, which gets burned when they don't get enough food. Not that the humps disappear after weeks in the desert, but they do get floppy and bounce from side to side.

A mastiff and a spaniel are two dogs that we know came over on the *Mayflower*.

Electric eels are not the only creatures that can generate electricity. Scientists know of about five hundred more.

An average-sized herd of cows can produce 450 gallons of methane gas a day. Lighting a match around that could be *cattleclysmic*.

The world's most successful mouser was a tortoiseshell cat named Towser, who reportedly killed nearly twenty-nine thousand rodents during twenty-four years of service at the Glenturret Distillery in Tayside, England— an average of three mice a day.

A reader asks: Do any other primates beside humans walk consistently on two legs? Yes, the gibbon does, holding its arms up and out for balance.

How do you cross a lion and a tiger? Very carefully. You can interbreed them, though they'd never do so in the wild. If its mom is a tigress, the result is a "liger"; if a lioness, the offspring is a "tigon."

"Cheetah" is the Hindi word for "spotted one."

The brightly colored Gila monster lizard from America's southwest may be pretty to look at, but its venom is more than twice as poisonous as the rattlesnake's.

The Iditarod is the annual dog sled race that runs from Anchorage to Nome, Alaska. It honors Alaska's most revered canine, Balto. In 1925, Gunner Kaassen and a canine team headed by Balto made the long, treacherous dogsled journey with lifesaving serum when a terrible diphtheria epidemic broke out in Nome.

Dogs can hear up to 45,000 decibels, cats up to 64,000, mice up to 91,000, bats up to 110,000, and porpoises up to 150,000. People don't even come close—their highest is in the low 20,000s.

An ostrich's eye is bigger than its brain.

When a kangaroo is born, its just a hairless fetus-like thing about the size of a small peanut. It manages to climb up into its mom's marsupium (pouch) and stay there for six or seven months before finally becoming a miniature version of its parents.

Although ostriches can't fly, they can outrun a racehorse.

Yes, it sounds rude, but goats with horns are officially called "buttheads." No, really.

If your cat is typical, it will blink about twice a minute.

Would you be surprised to hear that humans are more closely related to gorillas than gorillas are to monkeys?

In a lifetime, a good dairy cow will produce about two hundred thousand glasses of milk.

Goats are much easier to milk than cows: they're smaller, less temperamental, and fonder of people. Also, they have only two teats, cutting the work in half.

Early Egyptians tried to domesticate the hyena to solve their rat problem, but it didn't work out. They tried a small desert cat next, with much better success.

Gorillas don't need to drink water. They get all the moisture they need from the 50 pounds of vegetation they normally eat in a day.

Animals don't have to be burned in the branding process. Some ranchers use "freeze branding" on their cattle: the cold destroys the hair follicles' pigment-producing cells, turning the hair in the branded area permanently white.

Remember Koko, the gorilla that learned to communicate with humans by signing? Well, she went ape over the Mr. Rogers television show. When Koko finally got the chance to meet Fred Rogers in person, she wrapped her long arms around him and then— as she'd seen him do a hundred times on TV—she reached down and gently removed his shoes.

The power of marketing: "mohair" and "cashmere" both sound a lot better than "goat hair," don't they?

Forty percent of homes with at least one dog also have at least one cat.

Put them on very large scales and you'll find that the elephant is the heaviest land mammal, followed by the hippo in second place, and the rhino in third.

The offspring of a female horse and a male donkey is a mule. The offspring of a female donkey and a male horse is a hinny. Neither mule nor hinny can reproduce.

There really is an answer to the question, "Which came first, the chicken or the egg?" Chickens evolved from an early Indochina bird called the red jungle fowl. Somewhere along the line, one of these fowls laid a genetically mutated egg that hatched something more like a chicken than a red jungle fowl. Hence the egg came first.

BUGS

A cockroach can live for a week or so without its head. Unfortunately, a headless cockroach can't drink, so it will eventually die of dehydration.

Chinese farmers encouraged ants as a sort of natural pesticide, since a large ant colony can capture several million insects a year.

Mexican jumping beans jump because there's a caterpillar inside. The "bean" is from a shrub that grows south of the border, and the caterpillar eats out the inside, jerking now and again to scare away birds and other seed-eaters. Eventually, the caterpillar grows up and emerges from the seed as a butterfly.

The ant farm was invented in the same year as Raid insecticide. Coincidence? You decide.

Which has more legs, a millipede or a centipede? If you know the metric system you'd think that "milli" (1,000) should beat "centi" (100) by a factor of ten, but that would be wrong. Depending on the species, millipedes have between thirty-six and four hundred legs; centipedes have between twenty-four and two hundred.

It's only the female mosquitoes that suck your blood. They need the extra nutrients in order to reproduce. So what do male mosquitoes eat? Fruit juices, mostly.

 Ever seen a formicarium? Don't be too sure you haven't—it's the formal name for an ant farm. Here's an irony: the contraption that has enslaved billions of ants for the amusement of humans was invented on Independence Day 1956.

Hold the poison! In medieval times, ants in the house were considered a sign of good luck and abundance.

There are no wild silkworms anywhere in the world. The species has become completely dependent on humans for survival.

You can buy honeybees in 2- or 3-pound packages. How many honeybees in a pound? Depending on the size and breed, between four thousand and five thousand.

MOVIES & TV

Three Stooges fans know that Moe, Curly, and Shemp were brothers. Larry and Curly Joe were not.

Old film buffs have wondered for years how American actor Raymond Burr ended up in the classic schlock Japanese movie, *Godzilla*. It turns out his part was added in two years after the movie's Japanese release in the hope of cracking the American market.

The earliest silent films weren't shot in Hollywood, which was then just a sleepy farm community best known for its figs. Back then, the film capital of the world was Fort Lee, New Jersey, home of Thomas Edison's studio.

More people attended the opening of *Snow White* in 1937 than the opening of *Star Wars* in 1977.

Nineteen-fifties teen icon James Dean made only three movies in his life. Only one was released before his death.

The typical thirty-second commercial costs about as much to produce as the half-hour sitcom it interrupts.

Originally, the *Looney Tunes* character Tweety Bird was pink. Censors thought he looked scandalously naked, so his feathers were quickly changed to yellow.

A young Julie Andrews played the role of Eliza Doolittle in Broadway's *My Fair Lady*, but studio heads decided she wasn't a big enough star to play in the movie, so they replaced her with Audrey Hepburn. So, Andrews signed on for the Mary Poppins role and won the Oscar that year for best actress.

Does Steven Spielberg hate lawyers? The mechanical shark in *Jaws* was known behind the scenes as "Bruce," which was the first name of Spielberg's lawyer. And the first major character to get eaten by dinosaurs in the movie *Jurassic Park* was the lawyer.

When Marilyn Monroe was just a girl, she wrote in a school assignment that her goal was "to become a teacher and own a lot of dogs."

After snoozing through a screening of *Gone with the Wind* at the White House, President Franklin D. Roosevelt complained, "No movie has a right to be that long!"

More evidence that movies are better than ever: The F-word is uttered 257 times in *Pulp Fiction*.

In 1990, pollsters asked preschoolers who should be president. They overwhelmingly chose Mr. Rogers. We second that nomination.

One of Walt Disney's favorite hobbies was planning train wrecks on his half-mile of miniature train tracks.

Other names considered before settling on *Monty Python's Flying Circus* included *Gwen Dibley's Flying Circus* (honoring Michael Palin's boyhood piano teacher); *Owl-Stretching Time*; *A Horse, a Spoon, and a Basin*; *Bunn, Wackett, Buzzard, Stubble and Boot*; and *The Toad Elevating Moment*.

Way back in 1971, *Green Acres*, *Mayberry RFD*, *The Beverly Hillbillies*, *Gomer Pyle*, *Hee Haw*, and *Lassie* were all canceled on the same day by CBS.

Speaking of bad influences, the lead characters in *Casablanca* smoke a total of twenty-two cigarettes on-screen.

A 216-minute movie with a cast of thousands, yet not a single woman in a speaking role: that's one way of describing *Lawrence of Arabia*.

Dignified Alfred Hitchcock had not one, but three different nicknames. His parents called him "Fred." His classmates taunted him with "Cocky." His preferred nickname was "Hitch."

One of Marilyn Monroe's therapists was none other than Anna Freud, Sigmund's daughter.

According to Disney, there were 6,469,952 spots painted on the cartoon dogs in *101 Dalmations*.

"He's got to stop, he's seen us . . ." were James Dean's last words, seconds before plowing his Porsche into a car entering the highway. Ironically, a few days earlier he had filmed a traffic safety spot.

It took forty-eight pigs to film the movie *Babe*. All of them, say the producers, were saved from the slaughterhouse after the filming, and were allowed to live out their natural lives in peace.

ART

Of the many works of art displayed in the Louvre in Paris, only one is by an American artist: *Arrangement in Grey and Black, No. 1: The Artist's Mother*, by Massachusetts-born James Abbot McNeill Whistler.

The world's widest painting ever was *The Panorama of the Mississippi* by John Banvard, depicting the shore along the entire Mississippi River. Although touted as being "3 miles long!" the painting actually measured less than a quarter mile (1,200 feet). After the artist's death, the painting was chopped up and used as theatrical backdrops. No piece of it survives.

Artists in the 1800s added ground-up mummy powder to their paints, hoping that the magic that kept mummies fresh for that many years would do the same for their colors.

You know *American Gothic*, the painting of the father and daughter with a pitchfork? The people depicted were not really farmers. The man was artist Grant Woods's dentist; the woman was Woods's sister.

Talk about self-absorbed artists: Rembrandt holds the record for the most self-portraits by a famous artist. He painted sixty-two of them. Van Gogh comes in second with forty.

Vincent Van Gogh painted his starry night scenes by fixing candles to his straw hat.

If you're an art teacher, you should know that St. Luke is the patron saint watching over you.

Why did the artist Van Gogh cut off his earlobe? The usual reason—to impress some girl. He sent the eerie thing to a *fille de joie* named Rachel with a note: "Guard this object carefully." Her reaction to his lobe offering is an instructive lesson to Romeos everywhere: First she fainted, then she called the village constable.

Pablo Picasso swore that smoking saved his life. As the story went, newborn Pablo wouldn't breathe. An uncle blew cigar smoke into his lungs, causing the infant to choke, then breathe on his own. Picasso continued the habit later in life and smoked until he died.

"Take another ton of rock off Lincoln's nose!" To carve Mount Rushmore, artist John Gutzon Borglum stood at a distance giving instructions over a walkie-talkie to the guys on the mountain with jackhammers.

Michelangelo wanted to be buried in his home city of Florence. The Pope, however, insisted that his body be entombed in Vatican City. Eventually, Michelangelo's nephew stole the body and shipped it in an unmarked crate to Florence, where it remains to this day.

You know that statue of the sitting naked guy that we call *The Thinker*? Carved by Auguste Rodin, it was meant to be a depiction of Dante, author of *The Divine Comedy*.

We guess you've noticed that Mona Lisa has no eyebrows. This was not a slip-up by Leonardo da Vinci. It was the style of the day in Florence, Italy—women in the 1500s plucked their eyebrows off.

In 1911, the *Mona Lisa* was stolen from the Louvre in Paris. It was found twenty-seven months later when the thief tried to sell it to a dealer in Florence for a measly $100,000.

WRITING

Luckily, William Shakespeare inherited real estate and his acting career paid well, because the most he earned for writing a play was £8 ($1,325 in today's money), never making more than an annual income of £20 ($3,313) from his writing.

It's not easy waiting for fame and fortune. Novelist Frank Norris liked to recruit friends to point at him in restaurants and stage-whisper excitedly, "It's him!"

Not surprising in retrospect is that oh-so-gay Oscar Wilde's first fiancee, Florence Balcom, decided that the chemistry wasn't right between them. She went and married Bram Stoker, the author of *Dracula* instead.

In 1928, writer Evelyn Waugh married a woman named Evelyn Gardner. To avoid confusion, their friends called them "He-Evelyn Waugh" and "She-Evelyn Waugh." Mercifully—for everyone but He-Evelyn—She-Evelyn solved the problem a year later by running off with another man.

Edgar Allen Poe married his thirteen-year-old cousin.

William wasn't Mrs. Shakespeare's only son. He had three brothers, Gilbert, Richard, and Edmund.

How did Edgar Rice Burroughs come up with his hero's name "Tarzan"? At the time, he lived near the town of Tarzana, California, and decided he liked the name. (A myth has since sprung up that the town was named after the ape man, but that's exactly backward.)

Stephen King was just a teen when he had his first story published in 1965. It was picked up by *Comics Review* and was called "I Was A Teenage Grave Robber."

Inspiration comes from many sources. L. Frank Baum claimed to have gotten the name for his imaginary Land of Oz from a filing cabinet marked "O–Z."

Margaret Mitchell wrote only one book in her life, but it was quite a book: the hypersuccessful *Gone with the Wind*. Before that, her only writing experience was as a feature writer at the *Atlanta Journal*, using the name "Peggy Mitchell."

You can copyright all sorts of things, but you can't copyright the title of your book.

George Orwell received this note back from a publisher to whom he'd sent his *Animal Farm* manuscript: "It is impossible to sell animal stories in the U.S.A."

Historians tell us that Aesop, the guy with all those fables, probably didn't really exist. Writing in the first century AD, Greek writer Valerius Babrius combined Greek folktales with stories from India and invented a smart slave, Aesop, who supposedly told them.

The second-most-published playwright in the English language? Neil Simon. William Shakespeare's still number one with thirty-seven plays on the books.

Aspiring writers take heart: The Brontë sisters' first book was a collection of their poetry, which they self-published in 1847. Despite their combined literary efforts, they managed to sell only two copies.

Robert Louis Stevenson had a dear friend who complained that she never got a real birthday because she was born on Christmas. When the author died, he willed her his birthday.

Spy novelist Ian Fleming was also an avid birdwatcher. When he was casting around for an "ordinary-sounding" name for his new spy hero, his eyes landed on his favorite bird identification book: *Birds of the West Indies* by ornithologist James Bond.

Although you wouldn't expect it from his guns 'n' gals spy novels, Fleming also wrote the children's classic *Chitty Chitty Bang Bang*.

A survey in 1978 by PEN, the international literary organization, found that the median annual income earned by published writers was $4,700, with 68 percent making less than $10,000, and 9 percent earning nothing. The results were so depressing to its members that the organization didn't bother updating the survey in subsequent years.

When troublemaker Henry David Thoreau graduated from Harvard, he refused to take his diploma. "It isn't worth five dollars," he said, complaining that Harvard taught "all the branches of learning, but none of the roots."

Author Anthony Trollope worked for the British post office for thirty-three years. During that time he wrote four dozen novels by rising at 5:30 am and writing a thousand words before trudging off to work. He's still known for his writings, but within postal circles, however, his biggest claim to fame is that he invented the street-corner mailbox.

When he was a desperately poor child, Charles Dickens was forced to work at a shoe polish factory in London.

It's said that as many as a quarter of the U.S. population believes that Sherlock Holmes was a real person. Holmes's apartment at 221B Baker Street regularly gets letters from people who want his help.

Have you heard of author Alissa Rosenbaum? The author of *The Fountainhead* and *Atlas Shrugged*, she's better known as philosopher Ayn Rand.

Edgar Allan Poe only received $10 from the *New York Mirror* for "The Raven" when it was published in 1845. Allowing for inflation, this still only amounts to $178 in today's money.

We're betting this is why he was so prolific: Voltaire reportedly drank about seventy cups of coffee each day.

As far as anyone knows, Ann Bradstreet of the Massachusetts Bay colony was the first poet in colonial America.

Stephen King claims that he was inspired to become a writer as a child by Hugh Lofting's *Story of Doctor Doolittle*.

Please note that in ancient Greek mythology Atlas holds up the sky, not the Earth.

John Milton wrote *Paradise Lost* after he had gone completely blind.

Who says a tome by any other name would sell as sweetly? Author Margaret Mitchell's discarded title ideas for *Gone with the Wind* included *Not in Our Stars*, *Bugles Sang True*, *Milestones*, *Jettison*, and *Bah! Bah! Black Sheep*.

Samuel Taylor Coleridge wrote his famous poem "Kubla Khan" while high on opium.

Robert Lewis Stevenson wrote *Dr. Jekyll & Mr. Hyde* during a six-day cocaine binge.

Ken Kesey found fodder for *One Flew Over the Cuckoo's Nest* while working as an attendant in a mental institution.

Ernest Hemingway would use only #2 pencils when writing his first drafts.

The first typewritten manuscript ever submitted to a publisher was Mark Twain's *Life on the Mississippi*

(1883). Twain loved newfangled gadgets and was one of the first to buy a typewriter when they hit the market, which he dubbed a "curiosity-breeding little joker."

During his long decline, its been reported that beat poet Jack Kerouac's favorite pastime was sitting close to the TV while watching *The Beverly Hillbillies* and slugging whiskey from a bottle.

No, "Frankenstein" wasn't the monster's name. Victor Frankenstein was the scientist who figured out how to "bestow animation upon lifeless matter." Author Mary Shelley's monster was named only "Monster."

 # MUSIC

What do Allen Ginsberg, Dr. Timothy Leary, Petula Clark, members of the Radha Krishna Temple, and Tommy Smothers have in common? They sang with John Lennon and Yoko Ono on the recording of "Give Peace a Chance."

Like Elvis, Liberace had a twin who died during birth.

Who's the most recorded musician in history? No, not Elvis. Try the "Nightingale of India," Lata Mangeshkar, who over fifty years has recorded more than fifty thousand songs in twenty Indian languages.

The violin is not only the smallest and highest of the string instruments, but it was also invented before its modern cousins the cello, viola, and double bass.

We thought this was a more recent musical trend, but the term "hip hop" first appeared way back when Jimmy Carter was president, thanks to "Rapper's Delight" by the Sugar Hill Gang (1979).

Before Mick Jagger was a lifetime rock 'n' roller, he studied at the prestigious London School of Economics.

If you straightened out a French horn, the instrument would reach 22 feet.

Techno-musician Moby got his pseudonym honestly—his real name is Richard Melville Hall, and he's the great-great-grandnephew of Herman Melville, author of *Moby Dick*.

Elvis Presley didn't believe in encores. A few moments after Elvis walked offstage, a voice on the PA would announce to the cheering fans, "Elvis has left the building," and that was that.

Of the five original members of the Beach Boys, only one had ever surfed—drummer Dennis Wilson, who later drowned while swimming.

The first song played on MTV was "Video Killed the Radio Star" by the Buggles.

The first recorded singing commercial was issued on phonograph disk in 1921. It was for the soft drink Moxie.

Everyone probably knows that the Beatles made their first U.S. appearance on the *Ed Sullivan Show*. Not as many people realize that Elvis debuted on the *Steve Allen Show* and the Rolling Stones on the *Les Crane Show*.

Which song has the highest sheet music sales? It's not "Happy Birthday," "The Star Spangled Banner," or "Yesterday." It's "Yes, We Have No Bananas" by Frank Silver and Irving Cohn, which sold over half a million copies in its first few weeks of sale in 1923.

Doris Day's real name was Doris von Kappelhoff. She took her professional name from the song, "Day After Day."

Struggling musician John Lennon shoplifted the harmonica you hear him playing on the Beatles hit "Love Me Do."

We literally couldn't believe our ears when we heard that more than 2,200,000 Americans play the accordion.

Did you know that the Turtles were the first rock band to play at the White House? The year was 1969, and the event was Trisha Nixon's Masque Ball.

Tuning an orchestra right before the conductor appears has its own protocol: The first violinist stands and asks the principal oboist to play an A. The other players then adjust their instruments to match the oboe.

Charles Manson was not just a murderous cultist, he was a songwriter. Before he was arrested, the Beach Boys recorded one of his songs called "Never Learn Not to Love."

"Happy Birthday" is the most performed song of our time, Remarkably, it's still under copyright until the year 2010.

Before the Sherman brothers, wrote many of the Disney hits, including "It's a Small World" and the music for *Mary Poppins* and *The Jungle Book*, they wrote the classic hit "You're Sixteen (You're Beautiful, and You're Mine)."

You think its nice when contemporary musicians perform on cartoon soundtracks? It's an old tradition. For example, Louis Armstrong, Duke Ellington, and Cab Calloway were featured musicians on Betty Boop cartoons.

Rock historians tell us that the very first "bootleg" album was a collection of unreleased Bob Dylan songs called *Great White Wonder*. The year was 1969.

What's in a name? Before the classic girl group became the Shangri-Las with hits like "Leader of the Pack," they were the Bon Bons with flops like "What's Wrong with Ringo?"

In 1883, Arthur Sullivan was knighted by Queen Victoria. His musical partner, William Gilbert, however, had to wait until the queen died. She hadn't liked that his lyrics brutally satirized her governmental officials.

Don't expect to see a production of *The King and I* in Thailand. The country's still pretty sore at the inaccuracies and disrespect for their king in both the book and the play that was based on it.

"Scrambled Eggs" was the working title of Paul McCartney's "Yesterday," when all he had was a tune with no words. (The next line was, "Oh, my dear, you have such lovely legs.")

In case you're wondering, both the Hokey Pokey and the Bunny Hop were invented at Sun Valley Ski Resort in Idaho. And that's what it's all about.

MISCELLANEOUS

Add this to your "Major Character with the Fewest Lines in a Movie" list: in *Snow White*, Dopey utters just one thing in the entire movie: a hiccup, rendered flawlessly by voice artist Mel Blanc.

The oldest comic strip is *The Yellow Kid*, first published in 1896.

The most durable comic strip of all time? The *Katzenjammer Kids*, created by Rudolph Dirks in 1897, and still being syndicated 105 years later.

Professional clowns register their faces with a face registry so that no two clown faces are exactly the same.

Besides being creative people, what do Walt Disney, Ernest Hemingway, Dashiell Hammett, e.e. cummings, and W. Somerset Maugham have in common? All were ambulance drivers during World War I.

Dr. Seuss (Ted Geisel) created the first color animated commercial. This was for Ford in 1949.

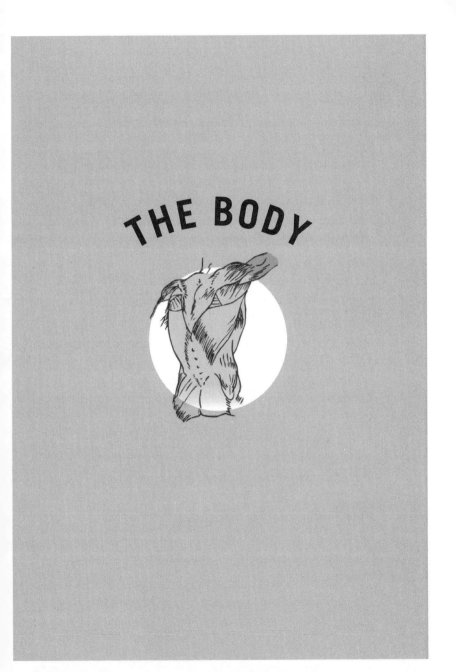

THE BODY

If you straightened out your digestive system from mouth to anus, it would stretch to the height of a three-story building.

The rumors are true: blondes have more individual hairs on their heads (about 140,000) than brunettes, who have only about 105,000. Redheads come in last with approximately 90,000.

According to Gillette, if you're male and didn't shave your face for sixteen years, you'd theoretically gain an extra pound in hair—a beard that runs about 30 feet long.

Did you know that if you're average, you have about 2 square yards of skin on your body?

Human eyes can see some seven million shades of color. Of all of them, lemon yellow is the most visible to the human eye. Red is the second most visible.

Which would kill you first—no food or no sleep? Most people could last for nearly a month without food, but would die after about ten days if not allowed to sleep.

Each of your eyeballs
weighs about an ounce.

Here's something to
make you squirm: there are little bugs that live in your
eyebrows and eyelashes. They're called follicle mites,
and nothing you can do will get rid of them. They're
actually pretty important, though. They eat away
dead skin and dust trapped between the hairs.

Your body may continue to grow, but your eyes have
reached their full size before puberty. As a matter of
fact, your retina finishes growing by about age two.

Hair on your scalp will grow approximately a half of
an inch per month.

Living in a right-handed world takes its toll on left-
ies: as a group, they incur more injuries than righties.

The little thing hanging in the back of your throat is
called a uvula. It helps keep you from gagging as you
swallow.

A good custom artificial eye, matching your natural color perfectly, will cost you from $1,700 to $2,400. But don't call them "glass eyes"—they're made from unbreakable plastic.

If you laid out your entire circulatory system in a straight line, it would stretch about 60,000 miles— enough to circle the globe two and a half times.

Ancient Greek physicians discovered that urine is sterile, so they began using it as an antiseptic on wounds. Because it worked so well to kill germs, it was used for many centuries as a toothpaste and dental rinse as well.

Your "funny bone" is called that only because somebody was trying to be punny: its real name is the humerus.

The Incas all had the same blood type (O positive).

Blood is always red, even if your veins look blue. In centuries past, European upper classes were pasty from being indoors, so their veins were more easily seen than those of the suntanned peasants. People assumed that their blood was blue, and that's where we got the term "blue bloods."

Hair is dead. Vitamins in shampoo do nothing for it.

Got hairy ears? Don't be shy. In India it's a measure of a man's virility, just as plumpness is the measure of wealth.

Heavy beer drinkers seldom get diarrhea. The beer irritates their stomachs into producing more acid, which kills the microbes that cause diarrhea.

According to the latest research, eating asparagus makes your urine smell strong. If you've never noticed it, it may be that you're one of the people who are genetically unable to smell it.

Rabies viruses travel slowly up the nervous system. How quickly an untreated rabies victim exhibits symptoms depends on the distance from the bite to the brain. For example, a bite on the neck might take three weeks, while a bite on the leg may take seven.

Scientists who know these things claim that the emotional centers of our brains more closely resemble the brains of cats than dogs.

What happens when you mix two incompatible blood types? In a beaker you can see the blood turn into globs of red, swimming in a pool of yellow liquid. In a person, it would bring on sudden death.

The very first artificial heart was implanted in 1969. The patient lived only four days.

Blood is said to be the most nutritious food in the world.

Dust mites live anywhere they can find dead skin cells—mattresses, pillows, carpets, the corners of your house. Most "dust allergies" aren't to dust per se but to these little arachnids that eat shed skin cells, which by the way, can make up to 70 percent of an average house's "dust."

Whether you're a genius or not, your brain weighs about 3 pounds.

Sword swallowers are not illusionists; they're actually swallowing the swords. They train to relax their muscles enough for the (blunt) swords to go all the way down.

In general, there are about ten thousand taste buds covering your tongue and the inside of your mouth.

If you're interested in things like muscle tone and bodybuilding, it may help to know that only 18 percent of skeletal muscle is protein. About 75 percent is water.

More than half of all your bones are in your feet and hands.

It was once believed that babies are born completely colorblind. This isn't so. Babies can typically see both reds and greens at birth. By the age of four months, they can distinguish all colors. By eight months, if given sufficient visual stimulation, babies can see about as well as adults.

The human heart beats an average of about one hundred times a minute. That's six thousand beats an hour, 144,000 beats per day, or 52,596,000 beats every year of your life.

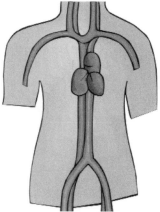

People who exercise regularly have a much lower heart rate than sedentary types.

If you ever have to choose between your left and right lung, keep the right. It has three lobes to take in air and exhale carbon dioxide. Your left lung, however, has only has two. Why? To make room for your heart and esophagus.

We've heard there's a word for the mush of food when it passes from your stomach into your intestines. It's called *chyme*. Furthermore, in the small intestine it turns into *chyle*.

Blood travels at about 0.7 mph. In twenty seconds, a drop of blood can circulate completely from the heart, through the body, and back to the heart.

The very first detailed and accurate anatomical drawings were not done by a doctor or scientist, but by an artist, Leonardo da Vinci, who used cadavers to detail the functions of the human body and its organs.

The life span of an individual eyelash is about 150 days, or a little under five months.

Got a pain in the neck? Appeal to Ursicinus of Saint-Ursanne, the patron saint of stiff necks.

Particles ejected during a sneeze have been clocked at speeds of up to 103.6 mph.

"Hallux" and the "minimus" are names for your big toe and little toe, respectively. We prefer the more technical terms, "this little piggy," and "that little piggy."

That little dip in the middle of your top lip? That's called a "philtrum."

If you're balding, stay in shape. Balding men often have higher levels of testosterone. Although this might be a good thing with the womenfolk, it can also mean a greater risk of high blood pressure.

Does size matter? A modern human has a brain that measures 1,200 to 1,350 cc. In contrast, brains of Neanderthals measured about 1,500 cc.

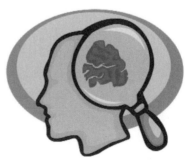

If it's any comfort on those hot summer days, it's not your armpits that smell. It's the excrement of the bacteria that live in your armpits.

How do antiperspirants work? They contain finely powdered aluminum or zirconium that get stuck in your pores so sweat doesn't escape easily.

The main gases that cause flatulence are nitrogen, methane, and hydrogen. Two of the three are flammable, and one is pretty smelly.

EVERYDAY THINGS

Pencils aren't hexagonal because it made them easier to grip. They were originally cut that shape to keep them from rolling off tables.

Swimsuits in the 1900s were made of wool and could weigh 20 pounds wet.

Manhole covers aren't round because someone at city planning liked the shape. Nope, they're round because a circle is the only common shape that won't fall through a hole if it gets tilted sideways.

Think of your day seeing outdoor displays, newspapers, magazines, radio, and television. If you're typical, you'll be potentially exposed to about three thousand ads today.

Before the invention of the razor, people used hammered metal, flint, and sharp shells for shaving.

Even the most avid comics readers don't know that Pvt. Beetle Bailey is brother to Lois Flagston from *Hi & Lois*. Mort Walker and Dik Browne created both strips.

A special edition of *Faust* by Johann Wolfgang Goethe printed in 1867 was the first known paperback book.

What we call "parchment paper" is a weak attempt to duplicate the look and feel of the real thing. Real parchment is not paper but the pressed skin of goat, sheep, or calf. It works poorly in an inkjet printer.

Almost everyone remembers the brouhaha created when an MTV interviewer asked presidential candidate Bill Clinton what type of underwear he wore, but few remember the answer. After a very long pause, he answered "briefs."

A quick primer on jigsaw puzzle terminology: A "nub" is a part that sticks out. A "void" goes in. Putting the right nub into the right void culminates in a "lock." Happy puzzling!

In the United States, more gold is used for manufacturing class rings each year than for any other category of jewelry.

Hold the mayo when you're polishing your silverware. It can dull knives and stain metal. However, some people swear that mayonnaise makes a great furniture polish and skin moisturizer.

The worldly Mark Twain once noted, "A soap bubble is the most beautiful thing, and the most exquisite in nature. . . . I wonder how much it would take to buy a soap bubble, if there were only one in the world."

The term "B. O." for "body odor" was coined in 1919 as an advertising gimmick for Odo-Ro-No deodorant.

In a sticky Silly Putty jam? According to our sources, isopropyl alcohol will remove the messy goo from most fabrics and carpets.

Thirteen tons of gold. That's the typical amount used by American dentists each year for fillings, crowns, and inlays.

The basic ingredient in bubblegum—polyvinyl acetate—is also used in the glue of U.S. postage stamps.

Mr. Potato Head used to have a pipe. Surgeon General C. Everett Koop lobbied Hasbro to get rid of it because it made the famous spud a bad example for kids. Hasbro complied in 1987, and Mr. Potato Head was appointed the "Official Spokespud" of that year's Great American Smokeout.

Experts say you should scrub for at least twenty seconds with soap and water for your hands to be considered sanitary.

The skin of a bubble's been measured. It's about a few millionths of an inch thick.

For your list of bad business predictions, add this one: "I think there is a world market for about five computers." —Thomas J. Watson, founder of IBM, 1943

Can you find the second Abe Lincoln on a penny? Look carefully at the back.

It was the Egyptians who can be credited with inventing sunscreen. Almost ten thousand years ago, ancient shepherds used crushed castor beans to block out the penetrating rays of the sun.

A 1956 advertisement for L&M cigarettes claimed the smokes were "just what the doctor ordered" to reduce coughs.

Have you ever wondered how they wind toilet paper neatly onto those 3-inch cardboard tubes? Actually, they don't. Manufacturers wind wide rolls of paper around long tubes, and then slice them into smaller rolls.

If you're average, you've got about twenty-five T-shirts in your drawer.

Kodak means absolutely nothing. It was chosen by George Eastman because it was easy to say and remember yet resembled no other word in the English language. The same is true with Sony and Exxon.

Levi's jeans once sported a rivet on the fly, when they first went on the market in the 1800s. That was until the company began receiving dozens of complaints from testy cowboys. It seems the tiny piece of metal was a mighty good conductor of heat when squatting before a campfire.

Advertising man Leo Burnett didn't just create the Jolly Green Giant character. He also was behind the Marlboro Man, Charlie Tuna, the Maytag Repairman, Poppin' Fresh, the Keebler Elves, and Morris the Cat.

To make an average-sized paperback book, it takes a block of wood about the same size.

If you want to work at Disney World, you'll have to know the lingo. An "imagineer," for instance, is a ride designer. All employees (even food servers and street sweepers) are called "cast members," who are expected to always remain "in character." And paying customers are "guests."

Cotton and linen—those are the fibers that give dollar bills their unique feel.

The image of Atlas holding up the world became a popular illustration for bound collections of maps. That is how the atlas on your bookshelf got its name.

How many ridges are there around the edge of a United States dime? 118. Don't believe us? Count 'em yourself.

In ancient China, the color of your fingernail polish was an indicator of your rank and position.

Government mints don't try real hard to make their coins pretty, for a simple reason: people keep the pretty ones, quickly taking them out of circulation.

Old Chinese coins had holes in the center for easy carrying. Like beads, they were easily strung together with a string. The idea is so good that the U.S. mint once considered doing the same.

The U.S. Postal Service happens to own the world's largest collection of rubber stamps.

Besides gold, silver, copper, and other metals, the following have been used as money through the centuries: velvet, beads, elephant tusks, bullets, playing cards, tobacco leaves, bat hair, cheese, shells, salt, beetle legs, and even gigantic stone wheels.

Maybe you've never heard of Hal Mason, but you probably know his work. He's the creator of ad icons Mr. Clean, the Raid roaches, and the Pillsbury Doughboy.

In a 1985 Procter & Gamble poll, 93 percent of the people polled could recognize Mr. Clean, while only 56 percent could recognize then vice president George H. W. Bush.

Dollar bills in typical circulation wear out after about eighteen months. Other denominations don't get as much day-to-day use, so they tend to last longer.

What's the year's longest month? October. Thanks to the daylight savings time adjustment, the month lasts thirty-one days and one hour.

Historians believe that bristled tooth-brushes were first invented in China during the fifteenth century.

By most accounts, Julius Caesar invented the practice of flipping a coin as a decision-making process.

Although it took decades to become a household fixture, the squeezable toothpaste tube was invented in 1892.

Alas, Joseph Rechendorfer's memorable name has been nearly erased from history. He's the guy who first thought of putting an eraser onto a pencil. Rechendorfer received a U.S. patent for his contraption in 1858.

You may snicker about the name of Ben Gay, but it's just the phonetic spelling for the name of French pharmacist Jules Bengue, who created it in 1898.

The first jeans with zippers came out in 1926, made by the Lee Jeans Company. Before that, it was buttons only.

A poll claims that 61 percent of all Americans like to hear music when they're put on hold, but that 22 percent prefer silence.

Why is that lubricant called WD-40? The WD stands for "water displacement," because it was first concocted to seal metal and prevent rust. The "40" honors the company's thirty-nine unsuccessful attempts to get it right.

Call them all "neon" lights if you want to, but it's only the red ones that contain neon. The yellow ones contain a sodium gas; the blue ones, mercury.

FOOD and DRINK

Licorice can raise your blood pressure.

How long ago did the Chinese start using chopsticks? The first known mention in print comes from about two thousand years ago, but historians think that their history goes back thousands of years before that.

The average American peanut consumer eats 3.3 pounds of peanuts a year.

Splurge with impunity: No matter what your mother told you, it's a proven fact that chocolate does not cause pimples.

Raisinettes, please! Movie theatre owners make the bulk of their money from selling snacks—more than $650 million last year.

It may surprise you to know that the stuff that goes into Spam isn't really that bad. It's mostly just pork shoulder—a cut of meat too fatty to be sold as ham, but not fatty enough to be sliced into bacon.

If life hands you peanut plants, make peanut butter. You can make thirty thousand peanut butter sandwiches from just one acre.

Don't age your rice wine. Unlike most other wines, sake is best when served fresh. Bonzai!

Back in the early days of soda, bottles were sealed with a cork. The sound of the cork gave soda its alternative name: "pop."

Americans consume coffee at the rate of 4,848 cups a second.

They're called "buffalo wings" not because they're made of American bison, but because the spiced and fried chicken originated at Frank & Teresa's Anchor Bar in Buffalo, New York.

The oldest known beer recipe was found on a Sumerian clay tablet dating from about 1800 BC.

One barrel of beer is equal to about 330 cans.

In old-time diner lingo, "Adam and Eve on a raft!" is how you order two poached eggs on toast.

In an average year, an average American will chow down on more than 20 pounds of candy, washed down with 56 gallons of sugared drinks.

Do you know what the pasta names mean in English? Spaghetti means "little strings," ravioli means "little turnips," linguine means "little tongues," fettuccine means "little ribbons," and vermicelli means "little worms."

Yes, you can overdose on caffeine. Ten grams could kill you. That's the equivalent of about one hundred average cups of coffee drunk in four hours.

Which cola has more caffeine, Coke or Pepsi? Coke has 46 milligrams in a 12-ounce serving; Pepsi has 38. Compare this to a cup of coffee (50–200 milligrams).

It was a dentist who first added sugar and flavorings to chicle to make chewing gum. That was Dr. William Semple in 1869. Perhaps he was trying to drum up business?

The average child eats 15 pounds of cereal a year.

Thirty-six dollars an ounce? No, don't call the vice squad, call the spice squad. Pickers pluck the stamens of nearly five thousand blossoms to get just one ounce of saffron, making it the most expensive spice on your grocer's shelf.

The Food and Drug Administration allows up to 210 insect fragments and seven rodent hairs in a regular 700-gram jar of peanut butter before considering the product too unsanitary for public consumption. The consuming public may have a differing opinion, of course.

You burn 1–2 calories per minute when watching TV. However before you decide to take it up as a weight-loss program, note that the average can of beer has 140 calories. That big bag of chips has about 1,600. You'd better get watching; it'll take sixteen hours to burn it off.

Way back in the 1930s when Pepsi first came on the market, it cost a nickel for a 12-ounce bottle. That sounds really cheap, but it's the equivalent of 50¢ in today's money.

To hard-boil an ostrich egg, set your egg timer for forty minutes.

Put a Twinkie snack cake in a microwave oven? Why would anybody do that? Nobody knows why, but those who have tried it tell us that in about 45 seconds, the Twinkie will explode.

O Power! The original name for Cheerios was Cheeri-Oats. Quaker Oats threatened to sue General Mills for using "oats" in the name, so the name changed and the cereal became a breakfast staple.

Foam on the range: root beer is deliciously foamier than other soft drinks because it contains extract from the yucca plant. Some of today's biggest root beer companies, though, don't see the importance in foam anymore, so have kept the yucca out. A representative of the Barq's root beer company went so far as to proclaim: "Foam is for shaving and birth control."

Ever see "carrageenin" on an ingredients panel and wonder what it is? It's a thickener used in lots of things like jams, puddings, dairy products, and fast food shakes. It's an extract made from red seaweed.

There really was a Maxwell House. It was a luxury hotel in Nashville, Tennessee.

A good batch of cider will not just contain one kind of apple, but a blend of three to five varieties.

Did you know that *fritos* means "fried" in Spanish? Fritos were named by an ice cream salesman named Elmer Doolin. When he tasted tortilla chips for the first time in a Mexican restaurant, he loved them so much he bought a tortilla factory from the owner. The rest, as they say, *es la historia*.

Betty Crocker never existed. She got her last name in honor of a former company director; the company added "Betty" because they thought recipes should come from a woman with a familiar and friendly name.

In the 1940s, Betty Crocker was voted the second best-known woman in America, second only to Eleanor Roosevelt. Not bad for a person who doesn't exist.

The Jolly Green Giant began his career as a scary-looking ogre wrapped in an animal skin. An artist gave him a kinder, gentler look that bean eaters everywhere continue to appreciate.

Lloyd's of London, famous for insuring the legs of Betty Grable and Bruce Springsteen's voice, was not started as an insurance company. Its founder, Edward Lloyd, began the business in the seventeenth century as a coffeehouse near the docks in London.

We may joke about the meat product Spam, but in Korea it has been highly prized. Seen as a luxury item, it was often given to newlyweds, coworkers, and business associates as gifts.

That flavor we call "bubblegum" is a mix of vanilla, wintergreen, and cassia (a form of cinnamon).

Three out of every four houses in the United States have at least one pack of Jell-O in the pantry.

In 1934, the National Biscuit Company took its basic cracker, removed the yeast, added extra shortening, liberally smeared it with coconut oil and salt, and named it after a grand hotel. The result? The Ritz Cracker.

To make one 12-ounce jar of peanut butter, it takes 548 average peanuts.

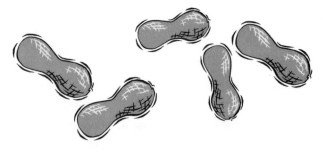

The Kennedy Biscuit company in Boston named cookies after local towns. Only one became a national hit—a fig-filled cookie named for Newton, Massachusetts.

An avocado is known in some circles as the "alligator pear."

The most popular condiment for a hotdog is mustard. After that, it's ketchup, onions, relish, chili, sauerkraut, and mayonnaise, in that order. Whereas 70 percent of hotdog eaters prefer more than one topping, there are still 7 percent of you who want your hotdogs plain.

The Aztecs believed chocolate would cure dysentery, act as an aphrodisiac, and, in large quantities, help you see the god Quetzalcoatl.

Thank a storm at sea that soaked coffee beans in saltwater for the accidental invention of decaf coffee.

There really was a Chef Boyardee . . . sort of. Hector Boiardi was a restaurant chef in Cleveland, Ohio, who began selling his pasta sauce on the side. When he expanded the business, he changed the spelling of his name so that Americans would stop mispronouncing it.

The Hershey's Kiss got its name because the machine that extruded the odd-shaped chocolates made loud "kissing" sounds.

In 1986, sausage makers in Barcelona, Spain, decided to see how long they could make a single sausage. They stopped at 5,917 feet (well over a mile).

Graham flour is just an alternative name for whole wheat flour.

Graham flour and graham crackers were both named after Sylvester Graham, a radical nutritionist of the 1840s. At a time when these were controversial ideas, Graham advocated taking baths, brushing teeth, eating whole grains and fresh vegetables, exercising, practicing family planning, and laughing at the dinner table to aid digestion.

The designer of the modern-day diner—P. J. Tierney—died complaining of stomach pains shortly after eating at one of his creations in 1917.

Pop-Tart flavors that saw a quick death in the marketplace included Chocolate & Cherry Chip, Frosted Peanut Butter & Jelly, and Chocolate Peppermint.

Ernest and Julio Gallo learned to make wine from a pamphlet they picked up at the Modesto public library.

In the early days before those pesky truth-in-advertising laws, Grape Nuts claimed it "prevents appendicitis," "cures malaria," "tightens loose teeth," and "heals tuberculosis."

The pressure inside a champagne bottle is about 90 pounds per square inch.

No surprise here: the average French person drinks about ten times more wine per year than the average American.

Not all dairy products are equal in doing a body good. An eight-ounce glass of skim milk has no fat in it. Eight ounces of whole milk has 8 grams of fat . . . and eight ounces of whipping cream contain 46 grams.

The "Melba" in Melba toast and Peach Melba was not the inventor, but Nellie Melba, a famous Australian opera singer in the late 1800s. The foods were created for her by an opera-loving chef named Auguste Escoffier during the diva's visit to the Savoy Hotel in London.

Weather patterns in 1828 resulted in extra-sweet grapes. More sugar means more food for the yeast. As a result, 80 percent of that year's champagne was lost in an epidemic of exploding bottles.

In the jungle, you should be alarmed if things suddenly smell as if you're standing in the lobby of a movie theater. When tigers mark trees with their urine, the smell is uncannily similar to buttered popcorn.

A recent poll in *Bartender* magazine found that lawyers and doctors are tied as the worst tippers of all professions.

The molded chocolate bar machine was invented in 1840, but caramel-manufacturer Milton Hershey didn't know they existed until he saw one in Germany in the 1890s. He immediately bought it. By 1911 he was making $5 million a year from his chocolatey sweets.

More artichokes are grown in California than any other state in the Union.

The colored and flavored gelatin you eat mostly comes from boiling cow bones and tendons.

Coffee "beans" are really the pits of a cherrylike fruit. How did people discover that coffee would make a stimulating drink? Coffee historians swear that a ninth-century Ethiopian goatherd saw his goats "dancing" after eating coffee cherries and tried them himself.

If blown into a cloud of dust near a flame, coffee creamer is very flammable. A fire-breathing dragon in the Disney theme parks is said to use Cremora for a nontoxic but impressive flame.

Kopi Luwak is the world's most expensive coffee at about $300 a pound. What makes it special is that the beans are recovered from the scat (excrement) of Paradoxurus, a tree-climbing marsupial that eats only the very best coffee cherries.

The Bible mentions two nuts by name: the pistachio and the almond.

McDonald's Hamburger University is the place where prospective managers can train in courses like Introductory French Fries and Advanced Burger Flipping.

The original name for the soft drink 7-Up was "Bib-Label Lithiated Lemon-Lime Soda." It contained lithium, still used as a powerful antidepressant, and was marketed as a pick-me-up. We guess so!

The dish succotash—that succulent mixture of corn and lima beans—comes from the Narragansett tribe. The name comes from the word *msickquatash*, which means "ear of corn."

Ketchup was never made with tomatoes until Americans tried their hands at it. The name comes from *ke-tsiap*, from the Chinese who invented it as a pickled fish sauce.

Native American George Crum, a resort chef in Saratoga Springs, New York, accidentally invented potato chips. Crum, exasperated by a diner who kept sending his french fries back for being "too thick," decided to slice the fries paper thin. Crum's attempt to rile the guy backfired when the diner thought the crisp potatoes were the best thing he had ever tasted.

Sure, stomping grapes for wine may look like fun, but it was really tiresome, tedious, painful work. Dangerous, too. The grape skins are slippery, and the fermenting juice gives off large quantities of carbon dioxide. Grape treaders would sometimes fall in and drown, or die of asphyxiation.

Each hard kernel of popcorn must have at least 13.5 percent water inside to explode just right.

One study has it that, to Americans, the odors of peanut butter and coffee are the two most recognizable scents.

Louis Pasteur first developed his pasteurization process as a way of keeping wine from spoiling. It wasn't until later that it occurred to him that the process would also probably work with other things, like milk.

The main part of a Cheeto is made of extruded, puffed cornmeal. It's then coated with that bright orange powder that's mostly cheese flavor and dyes. Mmm.

Curiosity killed Sir Francis Bacon. One freezing night in 1626, he went outside with a freshly killed chicken and stuffed it full of snow to test the theory that freezing could keep meat fresh. While the cold preserved chicken, it didn't do the same for Bacon. He got bronchitis and died two weeks later.

Until stopped by the government, soup makers photographed their soups with clear marbles in the bottom to push the meat and vegetables to the top. Now they get the same effect by using wide, shallow bowls.

 Why is it called "doughnut"? Before they evolved their holes, the deep-fried pastry started out as a little ball of dough the size of a nut. The shape changed, but the name remains the same.

The can had been around for forty-eight years before someone finally invented the can opener. A reader asks: "So what did people use to open cans in the half-century before the can opener was invented?" Whatever would do the job, but most often a hammer and chisel.

When did Orville Redenbacher first become obsessed with breeding popcorn? As a teenager in the 4-H Club.

Worldwide, what is the most popular kind of milk? Goat milk is first. Cow milk is second. Human milk is third (and especially popular among the younger set).

In an old-time diner, your waitress would shout to the cook, "Burn the pup, all the way!" if you'd ordered a hot dog with everything.

In the 1830s, ketchup became known as a cure-all medicine, sold as concoctions like "Dr. Miles's Compound Extract of Tomato."

"Belch water"? "Cow juice"? In diner lingo, those were the terms for soda water and milk.

In the 1657, a doctor wrote that coffee was good for "miscarriage, hypochondria, dropsy, gout, and scurvy. Makes skin exceedingly clear and white . . . it quickens the spirits, and makes the heart lightsome."

Mustard gas didn't really contain mustard. It just smelled like mustard.

At the diner, "Betsy in a bowl!" meant that you'd ordered beef stew.

GEOGRAPHY

Pungi are the pipes used by Indian snake charmers. The fakirs play and move rhythmically, and the snake moves to the tune. It's the movement, not the music, that makes the cobra "dance."

Only one state has no straight-line boundary: Hawaii.

Early Russian cosmonauts landed on solid ground instead of into the ocean like American astronauts. In 1965, *Voskhod 2* missed its planned landing spot, and the cosmonauts inside had to fend off hungry wolves for a day until rescuers reached them.

Half of Istanbul is below sea level.

The longest continuous part of the Great Wall of China is about 1,400 miles long. Despite what you may have read elsewhere, it is not the only human-made object you can see from outer space.

A reader asks, "Are there really places called Pago Pago and Bora Bora?" To which we can only reply, "Yes, yes."

Monaco, Nauru, and Singapore are countries that have no farms within their borders.

Where is the much-maligned town of Podunk? Massachusetts.

According to the people who keep abreast of unusual tourist attractions, the biggest fiberglass cow in the world is reputedly Salem Sue in New Salem, North Dakota. She stands 38 feet tall.

That's it? In all, only about 250 people through history have been recorded as having fallen from the Leaning Tower of Pisa.

The African country Mali gets its name from the Bambara word for hippopotamus. Its capital is Bamako, which means "crocodile river" in the same language.

Chang and Eng, the famous sideshow "Siamese twins" were actually only one-quarter Siamese, and three-quarters Chinese.

The ancient Hindus believed that sneezing drives away unwanted spirits trying to infest the body. After a sneeze, a sneezer would issue a quick blessing and snap his fingers to prevent the spirit from taking up a new residence in a bystander.

We call a holding cell "the drunk tank." The Japanese call it "the tiger box."

The largest McDonald's is in Beijing, China. It has two kitchens, twenty-nine cash registers, and seats for more than seven hundred people.

What's the only state with a one-syllable name? Maine.

The largest city in the United States can't be reached by car or train. It's Sitka, Alaska, covering 4,710 square miles on Alaska's panhandle, of which 1,816 are water. It's accessible by plane or boat only.

The ice sheet that covers Antarctica is roughly 6,500 feet deep. About 90 percent of the world's fresh water lies frozen there.

In terms of average wind speed, the windiest city in the United States is not Chicago, but Cheyenne, Wyoming.

The world's oldest restaurant is Ma Yu Ching's Bucket Chicken House in the city of Kaifeng, which opened in 1153 AD and still serves noodles and rice.

You probably already know that the South is called "Dixie" after the Mason-Dixon Line, but do you know why it's called that? Charles Mason and Jeremiah Dixon were English astronomers hired to settle a boundary dispute between Pennsylvania and Maryland in the 1760s. Years later, the border they drew also ended up being the boundary between free and slave states.

In September of 1781, a group of forty-four Mexican pioneers arrived at Nuestra Señora la Reina de Los Angeles de Porciuncula ("Our Lady the Queen of the Angels of Porciuncula") to build a village. As the village grew, they shortened the name to Los Angeles.

Neanderthal man was named after the Neander Valley in Germany. The valley was named after the seventeenth-century hymn writer Joachim Neumann, who used "Joachim Neander" as a sly pen name. Neumann means "new man" in German; "Neander" means the same thing in Greek. It was just a coincidence that people would discover a new species of humans in "New Man Valley."

The island of Madagascar smells yummy. More than half of the world's vanilla beans are grown there, resulting in an ice-creamy aroma.

Although Christopher Columbus never came anywhere close to Asia, he died believing all the places he'd landed in the Americas, were part of it.

The Great Chicago Fire of 1871 began in Mrs. O'Leary's cow shed and burned hot and fast for thirty hours, destroying much of the city and killing about three hundred people. While it got all the press, a much larger forest fire on that same day roared through Wisconsin and Michigan, taking more than a thousand lives.

Ever hear of the state of Franklin? It had its own constitution and state government for four years, but was never accepted by the Union. Finally, in 1788 Franklin disbanded, gave up its statehood dreams, and later became part of Tennessee.

You know the state flag of Alaska, showing the Big Dipper on a blue background? It was designed by a thirteen-year-old boy named Bennie Benson in 1926, thirty-three years before Alaska became a state.

What state's the fishiest of all? Maine. It produces more tins of sardines—about seventy-five million each year—than any other state in the Union.

Lincoln, Nebraska, boasts the world's only known roller skating museum.

The first jigsaw puzzles, created in the 1760s, were maps. It's a logical choice: cutting along boundary lines to teach geography.

Despite its name, Fort Worth, Texas, never actually had a fort, even though it was an Army post from 1849 to 1853.

"Old Folks at Home" by Stephen Foster is the state song of Florida, but it's not because of the large number of retired people there. Most people know the song by its famous first line: "Way down upon the Swanee River...."

 Cartographers tell us that the little directional indicator on a map actually has a name. It's called a "compass rose."

File for your next bar bet: a spot just north of Lebanon, Kansas, marks the exact center point of the contiguous United States.

A reader in Boone, North Carolina, wants us to illuminate readers to the fact that their fair town has been dubbed "the Firefly Capital of America."

Thousand Islands salad dressing got its name from its birthplace—the Thousand Islands of the St. Lawrence River, in Canada.

The only state capital in the country that made it into the twenty-first century without a McDonald's franchise is Montpelier, Vermont.

The first gold rush in North America took place not in California, but in Dahlonega, Georgia. The Spanish and Indians had gold mines there starting at least as far back as the 1500s.

More American soldiers have been killed in the state of Virginia than any other location worldwide. That's largely because most of the Civil War battles took place there.

The oldest town in America is Oraibi, Arizona. It was founded about fifteen hundred years before New York and is still inhabited.

Grand old party towns: Democrat and Republican are both towns located in North Carolina.

About half of all Americans live within 50 miles of their birthplace.

What country borders the United States besides Canada and Mexico? Russia. The U.S.-Russia maritime boundary zigzags down the Bering Strait. Alaska's land mass is less than 3 miles from Russia's, a short walking distance over winter's ice.

If you ignore the fact that nearly half of it is underwater, Hawaii's Mauna Loa is the world's tallest mountain. Measured from sea floor to its tip, it's 2,965 feet taller than Mount Everest.

The Pebble Beach golf course was founded by Samuel Morse, nephew and namesake of the guy who invented the telegraph.

Lake Chaubunagungamaug in Massachusetts has a longer name than any other American lake.

The United States isn't the only country that celebrates independence on July 4. The Philippines were granted political independence by the Americans on that day in 1946.

HISTORY

"You sock-dologizing old mantrap!" Those were the very last words President Abraham Lincoln ever heard. It's from the play *Our American Cousin*. Assassin John Wilkes Booth knew that actor Asa Trenchard's line always got a big laugh, and during the hilarity and applause, approached the president from behind.

In 1889, a congress of world socialist parties held in Paris chose May 1, 1890, as a day of demonstrations in favor of the utopian goal of an eight-hour working day (instead of ten to twelve hours, which was normal at the time).

Virginia Dare goes down in history as the very first European baby born in North America. The day was August 18, 1587. Three years later, however, little Virginia mysterious disappeared along with everyone else in the Roanoke colony.

The term "freelancing" dates from the twelfth century when knights who lost employment with royal houses offered themselves as mercenaries.

For several years after the Civil War, the best dentures were advertised as containing teeth yanked out of the bodies of healthy young soldiers who had been killed in battle.

Usual pay for a cowboy in the Old West was food, a place in the bunkhouse, and a dollar a day.

Before she was a master chef, Julia Child was a spy. She served in India and China during World War II.

It was sons of the rich and noble who became knights. You had to be rich—a suit of armor cost as much as a small farm.

Perhaps the Pilgrims were more like frat boys than we suspect: The *Mayflower* was supposed to land further south than Massachusetts, but as one passenger put it, "We could not now take time for further search, our victuals being much spent, especially our beere."

Plenty of bathrooms for a really stupid reason: the Pentagon has twice as many facilities as necessary because it was built during a time when Virginia law required separate bathrooms for blacks and whites.

Three hundred forty-two cases of tea were tossed into the harbor during the Boston Tea Party.

Smile when you say that, partner: Jesse James's nickname was Dingus.

French king Louis XIV prided himself on bathing once a year—that was a lot more frequently than most people bathed at the time.

Vice president Martin Van Buren was a gun-totin' man. As a matter of fact, he always had a pair of pistols beside him whenever he presided over the Senate.

Russian czar Peter the Great loved playing dentist, especially the part about extracting teeth. When his courtiers learned to stop complaining of toothaches in his presence, Peter began randomly choosing subjects for oral inspection.

How come the history books never mention Napoleon's ailurophobia (fear of cats)? Once in the midst of a war, he was discovered cowering in his tent. The object of his terror was a cute little kitten that had wandered in looking for some milk or a friendly lap. The invading feline was removed by an aide, and the shaken general got back to waging the war at hand.

Benito Mussolini was once a substitute teacher before he became the fascist dictator of Italy. Many school kids will tell you this makes perfect sense.

Because of opium's widespread use as a painkiller, more than a hundred thousand soldiers came home from the Civil War addicted to it.

On her way up the steps to the guillotine, Marie Antoinette accidentally stepped on the toe of the executioner. As a result, history records her last words as, "I am sorry, Monsieur. It was not intentional."

In 1731, the first public library in America opened its doors, thanks to the work of Ben Franklin.

Albert Einstein was a physics and mathematics teacher. He also said, "Education is what remains after one has forgotten everything he learned in school."

Prior to 1942, the Department of Agriculture gave subsidies to poppyseed growers to make sure that America didn't run out of opium derivatives.

For centuries, bathing was considered unnecessary, unhealthful, and even immoral. English diarist Samuel Pepys (1633–1703) noted with surprise that his wife, who had taken one bath in her life, was considering taking another!

The White House was originally gray. After the British Army set fire to the presidential mansion in 1814, it got a coat of white paint and a new nickname.

What kind of doctor was gunfighter Doc Holliday? That gun-slingin' pal of Wyatt Earp was a dentist.

Back in ancient Sparta, proud of its ruthless tactics in wars of all kinds, students took courses in subjects like deception, stealing, and killing.

Knights who served in the Crusades were buried with their legs crossed.

The strangest of unions can form in wartime. During the Crimean War, for example, nurse-pioneer Florence Nightingale's constant companion was a tiny pet owl she kept in her pocket.

The Pilgrims didn't really wear those buckles, dark clothes, and goofy hats. That was an invention from the 1800s. In reality, they dressed as everybody else did in Europe at the time, in a variety of colors.

Wall Street really had a wall running along it in the 1600s, designed to keep out animals and the British. It didn't last long—the British tore down the wall and took over the city, and bears and bulls have roamed the street ever since.

General George Washington was never shot in battle, but he had a couple of near misses when bullets pierced his coat and hat.

The deadliest natural disaster in the United States' history took place on September 8, 1900, as a hurricane struck Galveston Island, Texas, and killed eight thousand people.

On October 5, 1582, absolutely nothing happened. In fact, there was no such day. Over time the calendar had gotten ten days askew from the solar year, so Pope Gregory XIII eliminated October 5–14 to catch up.

Desiderius Erasmus (1466–1536) was the author of one of the earliest etiquette books, which included this advice about breaking wind: "Let a cough hide the explosive sound." Not like now, when you can just blame it on the dog.

The cost to send a half-ounce letter by Pony Express for a speedy eight-day delivery from St. Louis to Sacramento? Initially $5 (the equivalent of $95 in modern money), but with time, that dropped to $1 ($19).

After just one and a half years of existence, the Pony Express stopped running on October 26, 1861, two days after the transcontinental telegraph went on line.

On the streets of medieval Europe, if you heard someone call from an upper window, *"gardez l'eau!"* you'd best step aside. That was the warning call from someone about to dump their bedpan out into the streets.

John Locke helped mold the modern world's view of human rights. However, his *Thoughts on Education*, published 1690, was a little less inspired. It counseled bathing babies in freezing water, dressing them in thin-soled shoes so that water can leak in, quenching their thirst with beer, and never, never feeding them fruit or meat.

Ramses II, famous king of Egypt from 1279–1212 BC, sired more than 160 children. Ironically, this fact may have spawned the naming of the popular condom.

If you were brave enough to unravel a real mummy, despite the fabled curse, you'd discover that the cloth would stretch about half a mile.

Napoleon wasn't really that short. He was 5 foot 2, about average for French men at the time.

Besides bankrolling Columbus's expedition, what other thing did Spain's Queen Isabella and King Ferdinand do in 1492? Wanting to rule a "Christian nation," they forcibly exiled Spain's two hundred thousand Jews.

The brutal Spanish Inquisition—begun by King Ferdinand and Queen Isabella against Muslims, Jews, and other "infidels" in 1480—didn't officially end until 1834.

Some archeological discoveries are just accidents. A goatherd discovered the Dead Sea Scrolls. Preparing to demolish an ancient wall, engineers from Napoleon's army discovered the Rosetta Stone. Quarrymen discovered the remains of Neanderthal man. And a farmer digging in his vineyard discovered the ruins of Pompeii.

Military foibles: During World War II, the air division of the U.S. Navy accidentally bombed Boise City, Oklahoma. Oops.

Duck and cover! In 1958, a bomber jet accidentally dropped a nuclear bomb on Mars Bluff, South Carolina. Although it mercifully didn't explode, casualties included a church, several houses, and a garden.

Winston Churchill smoked about three hundred thousand cigars in his lifetime.

Pocahontas meant "playful one." When she converted to Christianity, Pocahontas took the name Rebecca.

Which came first, books or libraries? Libraries, actually—long before the first books were bound; early Egyptian libraries lent out literature that had been pressed onto clay tablets.

Although the Eiffel Tower is now beloved by Parisians, it was not always so. When it was finished in 1884, the outraged citizens called it an eyesore and said it looked like a "tragic lamppost." One citizen even dined every day in its restaurants, reasoning that it was the only place in Paris that you could sit and not see the tower.

About two thousand slaves, promised their freedom by the British, fought against the Americans in the Revolutionary War. This included twenty-two who ran away from Thomas Jefferson's plantation to join the British Army.

Enslaved people fought on the American side, too. However, despite fighting bravely, they were not given their freedom at the end of the war.

In 1870, Georgia was admitted for the third time to the United States. It had been readmitted in 1868 after losing the Civil War, but it was expelled again in 1869 because it had refused to ratify the Fifteenth Amendment (making it illegal to deny the vote to nonwhites).

On July 1, 1898, Teddy Roosevelt became a national hero (and eventually president) at the Battle of San Juan Hill. Despite the battle's name, his Rough Riders actually charged up Kettle Hill. Someone misread the map and the name stuck.

Besides bifocals, the Franklin stove, and the electric kite, Benjamin Franklin's firsts include America's first fire brigade, postal system, antislavery organization, and hospital.

So many Japanese volunteered to be suicidal kamikaze pilots as the war turned against Japan that authorities began only accepting those with the highest grades in school.

Westward slow! Wagon trains heading west averaged only about 1–2 mph, the equivalent of a toddler's walking speed.

KID STUFF

Complaints about schools likely go back to their beginning. Here's an inscription found in Nippur, Iraq, on a clay tablet from about 1700 BC: "The fellow in charge of Sumerian language studies said, 'Why didn't you speak Sumerian?' and caned me. My teacher said, 'Your handwriting is unsatisfactory' and caned me. I'm beginning to hate the scribal arts."

Early in its history, a Hamm's Beer advertisement claimed that it was good for putting kids to sleep.

Garfield's comic strip creator, Jim Davis, graduated from the same high school—Fairmount High in Fairmount, Indiana—as silver screen legend James Dean.

Popsicles were originally going to be called Eppsicles, named after their inventor Frank Epperson—a combination of "Epperson" and "icicle." His kids started calling them "Pop's Cycles," and the name more or less stuck.

If the classic Barbie doll were human, her measurements would be just a tad weird: 38-18-28.

If you need more evidence that you don't have to be smart to be president, consider this: grade-school dropout President Andrew Jackson loudly proclaimed his belief that the world was flat.

Adolf Hitler was the inspiration for the Dr. Seuss character Yertle the Turtle. Before his death, Seuss also admitted that Richard Nixon was the inspiration for *Marvin K. Mooney, Will You Please Go Now?*

Hunters in the Philippines once used yo-yos to snare an animal's legs and bring it down for the kill. The name "yo-yo" in the native language Tagalog means "come back" (literally "come-come").

What distinguishes gourmet jellybeans from the regular variety is that a little bit of the real food (cherries, peanut butter, jalapeño peppers) goes inside the candy bean.

Bozo the Clown wears a size 83AAA shoe.

We guess that could drive anyone a little batty: Batman took up crime fighting because as a child he witnessed the murder of his own parents during a robbery.

The Little Mermaid was originally Hans Christian Andersen's, not Disney's. As a matter of fact, Disney used a bit of creative license with its rendition. In the original ending, Andersen's mermaid turned into sea foam and blew away.

How good are obstetricians' estimates of the date of a baby's arrival? Not so good. Only about one baby in forty arrives on the due date. Of the rest, twice as many babies are born after the due date than are born before it.

In 1932, Ole Kirk Christiansen needed a name for his new toy company. He took inspiration from *leg godt*, the Danish words for "play well," and called his company LEGO.

In 1906, Frank Fleer invented bubblegum and gave it the catchy name of "Blibber-Blubber." However, it never quite reached the shelves because of one tiny glitch: The stuff was so gummy that only scouring and turpentine could remove it from skin. It was another twenty-two years before the sticky problem was (mostly) worked out.

Do you know what gives crayons that distinctive smell? Beef fat.

Remember the notorious "this is your brain on drugs" commercial? Researchers discovered an unintentional side effect when it ran—small kids refused to eat fried eggs, believing them to be somehow laced with drugs.

Illinois Avenue is the space most often landed on in Monopoly. Next most common are B&O Railroad, Free Parking, Tennessee Avenue, New York Avenue, and Reading Railroad.

What makes a daughter self-confident and personally successful? According to recent studies, a close relationship with her father, above all else, gives her a head start in life.

Pinball game designers keep this in mind when creating a new pinball game: An okay player should get an average of about forty-seven seconds of play per ball. Too much more time and the machine loses potential revenue; less, and the player feels defeated enough to stop playing.

Hoping to get a positive answer from your Magic 8-Ball? "CHANCES ARE GOOD." Of the twenty possible answers, only five are negative. Ten indicate "YES." The remaining five? They tell you to "ASK AGAIN."

If you've got a new box of crayons, expect the black one to get used up first, then the red. Those are the two colors that see the most wear.

A researcher asked kids which season is most boring. Fifty-three percent said summer.

The ratio of Barbie dolls to Ken dolls sold each year? Roughly two to one.

We know that Smoky Bear's middle name is "The." And Rocky Squirrel's middle name is "J." But Donald Duck's is more obscure. It was revealed on his enlistment papers in a wartime cartoon that his middle name is "Fauntleroy."

Remember Pac-Man? The name comes from the Japanese word *paku*, which means "eat."

It won't hurt you to do it, but we recommend that you don't crack open your Etch-A-Sketch to see what's inside. The silver stuff is ground aluminum that's so fine that it'll stick to anything it comes in contact with.

Mortimer Mouse was Mickey Mouse's original name.

Mickey Mouse was not Walt Disney's first big cartoon success. While working for Universal Studios he created a wildly popular character name Oswald the Rabbit. Universal was stingy with the profits, so Disney walked away to form his own studio.

Nintendo goes back a long way—more than one hundred years. At that point, though, the company wasn't making video games but playing cards.

Although Snoopy's litter had eight puppies, only six were named in the comic strip: Snoopy, Spike, Belle, Marbles, Olaf, and Andy.

"You have 'em, I'll amuse 'em." That's what Theodor (Dr. Seuss) Geisel said about having kids. He never had any of his own.

More flying discs are sold annually than basketballs, footballs, and baseballs combined.

According to math and card experts, a deck needs to be shuffled seven times to adequately randomize the cards.

It was the movement people used while twirling the Hula Hoop that inspired the dance, the Twist.

The real Christopher Robin, son of author A.A. Milne, grew up hating the Winnie the Pooh stories because of the notoriety and ridicule from peers they caused him.

A.A. Milne, for his part, grew to wish people would pay less attention to his Pooh stories and more to his *real* writing—serious plays for adults.

When the 3 Musketeers Bar debuted in 1932, its name almost made sense. Back then, the bar divided into three pieces with chocolate, vanilla, and strawberry inside. In 1940, it dropped the vanilla and strawberry, but the name remained the same.

Chinese checkers are not really Chinese. The game was invented during the 1880s in jolly olde England.

Who was Mother Goose? Nobody really knows, but the legendary storyteller's name was known in France during the 1600s and first appeared in print in 1697, thanks to a book by folklorist Charles Perrault.

They weren't always Frisbees. When Wham-O introduced its flying disc in 1957, they called it the Pluto Platter.

Clowns can protect their faces from being copied by sending a small fee and photo of themselves to the National Clown and Character Registry. For archival purposes, the registry then paints each clown's distinctive face onto a goose egg.

According to the employee manual, Walt Disney himself would have been forbidden to work at one of his own theme parks. Mustaches and beards are not allowed.

Even author E.B. White became teary-eyed by the death of his fictional spider Charlotte. When he recorded the book *Charlotte's Web* on tape, it took nineteen takes before he managed to read that part without his voice cracking.

Hans Christian Andersen was deathly afraid of being buried alive, so he left notes around his bed saying that he only "seemed dead."

¡Olé niños! ¡Magnifico! Did you know that the kids song "La Cucaracha" is about a cockroach who wastes his life away smoking marijuana, then dies, and is carried away to be buried by buzzards and a church mouse? Now you do.

During the worldwide cartoon craze of the 1930s, even Emperor Hirohito of Japan reportedly sported a Mickey Mouse watch on his wrist.

Modern-day circuses were fashioned after the circular Roman coliseum. As a matter of fact, the word "circus" comes from the Latin, meaning "round."

In the year 2000, the LEGO company manufactured 306 million tires for its construction sets and publicly claimed the distinction of being "the largest tire manufacturer in the world."

During Bugs Bunny's long career, both the Broccoli Institute of America and the Utah Celery Company lobbied hard to get the rabbit to switch to their vegetables. To no avail—carrots remained the cornerstone of the comic hare's routine.

Each year, the average American kid eats more than 15 pounds of cold cereal.

Everyone's familiar with circus king P.T. Barnum. You may know he coined several words and phrases in his younger years like "Siamese twins," "jumbo," and "The Greatest Show on Earth." But few recall that he spent his later years as a Connecticut legislator, the mayor of Bridgeport, Connecticut, and a Temperance lecturer.

By the way, despite numerous attributions, there's no evidence that P.T. Barnum ever said, "There's a sucker born every minute."

A reader asks: "Whatever happened to Batman's sidekick, Robin?" There have been three different Robins in the comic books. The first grew up, split from Batman, and became superhero Nightwing. The second got caught in a warehouse explosion, and a phone-in poll of readers decided he should die. The most recent Robin is still around—for now anyway.

Bullwinkle the Moose was named after a Berkeley, California, auto dealership, Bullwinkel Autos. His creator, Berkeley native Jay Ward, speculated what a guy with that name would look like, and a big dumb moose was the result. The auto dealer, Clarence Bullwinkel, was a Republican politician and didn't look at all like a moose.

On average in the United States, by a child's tenth birthday, he or she will have used up almost 11.5 boxes of 64-count crayons. That averages out to about 730 crayons.

The original 1952 Mr. Potato Head came with no body, just a Styrofoam place holder that held all the attachments until you could find a real potato and begin play.

Bud Abbott, of Abbott & Costello fame, was literally born in a circus tent. He had a father who was an advance man in the Barnum & Bailey circus and a mother who rode elephants under the big top.

What a doll! Barbie's first car was a 1962 pink Austin-Healey.

Love to yo-yo, but hate the sore fingers? Amateurs apply a Band-Aid to their yo-yo finger, but pros just tough it out. Finger calluses eventually form and become a badge of honor.

In Germany of old, pediatric specialists suggested using sheep brains to sooth a teething baby's gums.

You've probably guessed that marbles originally got their name because in the eighteenth century, they were actually made of marble.

Dr. Seuss finally became a real doctor in 1957 when Dartmouth gave him an honorary degree.

Ever wonder where whoopee cushions, sneezing powders, dribble glasses, joy buzzers, peanut-brittle snake cans, and snapping gums originated? Try Neptune, New Jersey, home of the century-old novelty giant, S.S. Adams Company.

Long before Mr. Potato Head there was the "Potato Head Blues," a hit for Louis Armstrong in the 1930s using a slang term for someone of low intelligence.

Designing things for a dollhouse? They're usually built at a 12:1 scale. That sounds complicated, but here's an easy rule of thumb: One inch in the real world equals one foot in the mini-world.

Mount Rushmore made of LEGOs? The 1:20 scale replica took 1.5 million bricks, report the folks at Denmark's Legoland.

"Jack" and "Bingo" are the names of the boy and dog pictured on the Cracker Jacks package.

Thirteen-year-old Antonio Gentile designed Mr. Peanut in 1906. The Planters Peanut Company gave him $5 for it.

Did you feel lost in the teeming hoards at your high school? It could've been worse. You could've gone to dear old Rizal High School in Manila in the Philippines. It's the world's biggest high school—in a recent year, 19,738 students attended it.

LANGUAGE

It's not what you think. The "poop deck" is located at the back end of a ship, and the term comes from the Middle French word *poupe*, meaning "stern."

If your phone number spells out a word, it's called a "numerym."

In case you want to impress a grammar teacher, the little dot on the *j* and *i* is called a tittle. (You there, in the back row—stop smirking!)

Have we mentioned, you're an ailurophile if you love cats?

Joseph Stalin wasn't the Soviet leader's real name. Stalin means "man of steel" in Russian, which we guess sounds better than the guy's real name, Iosif Dzhugashvili.

Paul Revere's French father changed the family name from Rivoire "so that the bumpkins should pronounce it easier."

The word "robot" came from a 1921 Czech play titled R.U.R. (Rossum's Universal Robots). Its author—Karel Çapek—created the word from the Czech word meaning "working."

Enter the Jargon: Keystones. Quoins. Dentils. Lozenges. Garlands. What's the subject? Architecture.

The word "bedlam" came from the lower-class British pronunciation of the name of an early mental institution: Bethlehem Hospital.

"Maudlin" came from corrupting the French pronunciation of "Mary Magdalene," who was often depicted in church art with eyes red and teary from weeping.

Pumpernickel bread is so hard to digest, even its originators called it rude names. In German, the name translates to "the devil's fart."

We've all had it on exam day: scholionophobia is an overwhelming fear of school.

There's a precise and polite word for dog poop: "scumber." Unless, of course you're talking about the poop of wild dogs—that's called "lesses."

The large wigs worn by men and women in eighteenth century Europe were called "perukes." They and the elitist behavior of those who wore them inspired the term "bigwig."

Xerography is what it's called when you make a photocopy of something. The word is Greek for "dry writing."

Would it be fun to be a funambulist? Well, maybe. A funambulist is a tightrope walker.

Don't ask us why, but "crocodile" comes from the Greek *krokodilos*, which means "worm of the pebbles."

By the way, if you deliberately eat bugs you're an entomophagist.

"Idiot," "moron," and "imbecile" are now just insults, but they were once legitimate medical classifications. Morons were said to have the emotional and mental capacities of nine-year-olds; imbeciles, five-year-olds; and idiots, two-year-olds.

Before educator Friedrich Froebel coined the word kindergarten (children's garden), he called his new classroom *kleinkenderbeschaftigungsanstalt* (institution where children are occupied). The name didn't catch on for some reason.

You may know that red herrings are smoked herrings and that they're pretty stinky. But did you know that escaped prisoners once effectively used them to throw tracking dogs off their scent. That's how "red herring" came to mean "diversionary tactic."

Confused about the difference between molybdomancy and myomancy? We're not surprised. Molybdomancers tell the future by dropping melted lead into water; myomancers tell the future by watching the behavior of mice.

Why are they called "sardines"? Because the process of canning small herrings was invented on the Italian island of Sardinia.

Competent writers know that "e.g." means "for example" and "i.e." means "that is" and never confuse the two in their writing. However it's a sure bet that few know that the abbreviations stand for the Latin *exempli gratia* and *id est*.

The oldest letter in our alphabet is *O*, first used by the Egyptians in about 3000 BC.

You've probably heard the term "shyster," which means an unscrupulous lawyer. The word most likely comes from the word shy. Early on, the word shy meant "disreputable," not "quiet" as it does today.

The newest letters in the alphabet are *J*, *U*, and *W*. *J* was derived from *I* in about 1600. *V* had double-duty as vowel and consonant until someone got the bright idea to round the bottom to create a *U* and double it up for a *W*. This happened during the Renaissance.

In a poll, American speech teachers came up with the ugliest-sounding words in the English language. The list included plump, gripe, sap, jazz, crunch, treachery, cacophony, phlegmatic, plutocrat, and flatulence.

The word "hurrah!" comes from the Norse "Huzzah!" It meant "On to paradise!" and was shouted as Scandinavian warriors raced into battle, and often to their deaths.

"Nile" in ancient Egyptian meant "water."

The word "Sunday" doesn't appear in the Bible at all. Not once.

Mark Twain once astutely noted, "The road to hell is paved with adverbs."

In 1825, John Quincy Adams installed the first toilet in the White House, leading to much commentary, many jokes, and the adoption of "Quincy" as a slang word for toilet.

Give a cheer for humorist and illustrator Gelett Burgess. His two claims to enduring fame: He coined the word "blurb," and in 1896, wrote the immortal verse: "I never saw a purple cow / I never hope to see one / But I can tell anyhow / I'd rather see than be one."

While it's true that no word in the English language will rhyme perfectly with "purple," some poets have tried to stretch the rules slightly and use a word like "burp'll." Likewise "orange" and "door hinge."

Can you perform *chantepleure*? It means "to sing and weep simultaneously"—a talent much prized in opera.

The word "idiot" is from the ancient Greek *idios*, which means "one of a kind, peculiar."

In the circus, a toilet is known as a doniker.

"I am about to or I am going to die. Either expression is used." Those were the last recorded words of Dominique Bouhours, a grammar expert.

 Sports linguists tell us that "golf" came from the ancient Scottish word *gowf*, which means "hit."

Odds are that if you counted all the letters in your newspaper, 13 percent of them would be *E*s.

The "Pennsylvania Dutch" aren't really from Holland. When asked their nationality, the newcomers said that they were *Deustch* (German). Americans—never very good with languages—completely misunderstood.

"Mush!" means giddyup to a sled dog, but it has nothing to do with hot cereal. It comes from French trappers shouting *Marchons!* ("Let's go, hurry up!") and English speakers mutating it to "mush on" and then just "mush."

William Shakespeare is sometimes credited with coining more than ten thousand words, from "assassination" to "zany." However, if he'd just made words up, it's unlikely that his audience would've understood his plays. More likely the words were already used conversationally and he was merely the first to publish them.

Let's not get them confused: Digamy means remarriage after divorce. Deuterogamy means remarriage after the death of a spouse.

Norman Mailer coined the word "factoid" in his 1973, book *Marilyn*. However, although the world adopted his word, it didn't quite adopt his definition: "Facts which have no existence before appearing in a magazine or newspaper, creations which are not so much lies as a product to manipulate emotion in the Silent Majority."

What does "pack my box with five-dozen liquor jugs" have in common with "the quick brown fox jumped over the lazy dogs"? Both are a "pangram," which means that they use all the letters of the alphabet.

Credit the unsung writers of newspaper headlines with coining such space-efficient terms as flu, veep, prof, prez, A-bomb, polio, quake, and champ.

If you want to impress an ornithologist, don't call it a "flock of flamingos," call it a "pat of flamingos."

Although "cobweb" comes from the Middle English word *coppe* meaning "spider," not all spiders build messy webs in dark corners. Cobweb spiders have clawlike legs and bulbous bodies. The most notorious is the black widow.

If you have chrematophobia, you have a fear of money.

In the mid-1800s, a famous trapeze artist—Jules Leotard—began wearing skintight, thin bodysuits to make his tricks easier for him to perform. Soon other high-flying performers were wearing similar suits, but they were so associated with Leotard that the name stuck.

Here's a tasty little morsel: hors d'oeuvre literally means "outside of work." It loosely means any food outside of the main course.

A reader wants to know, "What's the scoop on the phrase 'scot free?' Why pick on the poor Scots?" Actually, the word was adopted from the Old Norse *skot*, meaning a tax or contribution. It had no apparent relation to the haggis-eating, kilt-wearing bunch.

Next time you call your brother-in-law a "blockhead," you're honoring history. Originally, blockheads were wooden stands for hats and wigs. Some seventy years before the Pilgrims landed in the New World, "blockhead" was already being used as an insult in England.

"Coward," has nothing to do with cows. It comes from the Old French *couard*, meaning "tail," and referring to the image of a retreating dog with its tail between its legs.

The term "guerrilla" has nothing to do with the furry primate. It's Spanish for "little war."

It was a sweet Indian reed named *kand* that gave us the word "candy," after Alexander the Great carried the treat back to Macedonia in about 340 BC.

The name "raccoon" comes from a native American word *arakum*, which means "he scratches with his hands."

About five hundred years ago, someone came up with the idea of taping official documents together with red binding. This spawned the use of our phrase "red tape."

Ambrose Bierce defined litigation as: "a machine which you go into as a pig and come out as a sausage."

Anglo-Saxons covered their cold hands with heavy leather they called *glof*, a word meaning the palm of their hand. From this, we got "glove."

A round window is called an oculus (Latin for "eye").

Croquet and crocheting are related, sort of. The French thought that the game's wickets looked like crochet hooks.

By the way, "crochet hook" is redundant: "crochet" means "hook" in French.

The words "beatnik" and "hippie" were both coined by San Francisco newspapermen. The first by *San Francisco Chronicle* columnist Herb Caen in 1958; the second by *San Francisco Examiner* writer Michael Fallon in 1965.

Croatian soldiers of the mid-1600s sported scarves around their necks, a forerunner of the modern tie. The French loved the look and called the neckwear "cravats."

The word "nerd" first appeared in *If I Ran the Zoo* by Dr. Seuss. It was an animal, though, not a geeky fellow.

Linguists know of at least 133 Native American languages.

The average American reads 150–200 words per minute.

LAW

Considering how many trials there are in the United States legal system, it's staggering to realize that only 3 percent of all cases ever actually make it to the courtroom.

In an average year, the United States has about forty thousand liability lawsuits filed. Britain has about two hundred.

Thomas More is the patron saint of lawyers. For what it's worth, he's also the patron saint of politicians.

Switzerland didn't allow women to vote until 1971.

Did you know that the wheel is a patented invention? Not by Neanderthal man, or even by those legally shrewd ancient Babylonians, but by an Australian lawyer. He filed for the patent in 2001 to show that his country's new patent law was flawed. The patent office proved his point by granting the patent.

Those in the know claim that crows make very good house pets, but don't try it out. It's a criminal offense to own one without a special license.

Courts have ruled consistently that drunk driving laws apply to people riding horses, too. Rider and horse must be sober.

Peter the Great, working to modernize Russia, passed a law that men with long whiskers had to pay a special tax.

Because of "Blue Laws" forbidding such things on the sabbath, pro baseball didn't start playing Sunday games until 1933. Not that the laws changed—the baseball leagues just decided to ignore them.

Hey, now it can cost an arm and a leg! Hammurabi's Code of Law, enacted in 1780 BC in Babylon, dictated that a doctor found guilty of malpractice was to have his hands chopped off.

Women could not legally practice law in the United States until 1872.

Ever hear of the "lawyer bird"? The North American black-necked stilt is called that because one of its identifying features is *a big bill.*

How's this for election reform? Ancient Athens chose its five hundred lawmakers by lottery. They served a year, and then were replaced by the next year's winners.

It was illegal to play pinball in the city of Chicago up until 1976. This was somewhat ironic, since most of the major pinball manufacturers operated out of the Windy City.

An old French proverb states, "Men make laws, but women make morals." We're not dumb enough to get in the middle of this one.

St. Ives, another patron saint of lawyers, is often depicted with a cat—artistic shorthand to suggest a certain amoral opportunism.

Everyone knows that Aaron Burr shot Alexander Hamilton to death during a famous duel. What isn't always told is that they had first been law partners, setting the stage for their animosity.

Some say they had the right idea: after their respective revolutions both Russia and France tried hard to eliminate the practice of law.

Plato was a proponent of animals in the courtroom. He believed that every trial should have a dog present as a lie detector, because he believed that dogs could tell when someone was lying.

James Rodgers, a murderer sentenced to the firing squad, was asked if he had a final request. Said he: "Why yes—a bulletproof vest."

Judges in ancient China hid their reactions from courtroom attendants by wearing smoky tinted glasses.

Big court award? Don't start spending the money yet. If you're average, legal costs will eat up 54 percent of it.

A police detective shared what he takes to the scene of a murder: chalk for body lines, rubber gloves, a tape measure, a small penlight, manila envelopes, a small notebook, tweezers, and a jar of Vicks Vap-O-Rub to rub under his nose in case there are any nauseating smells.

Roger B. Taney, who served from 1836–1864, was the first Supreme Court justice to wear trousers under his judicial robes. Before that justices all sported knee breeches.

For many years, branding was considered an acceptable punishment for crimes. The last American to be branded was Jonathan Walker, whose hand was burned with the letters *SS* in 1844. He had been convicted of helping slaves escape; the initials stood for "slave stealer."

Perhaps one was a stool pigeon? In 1963 a court in Tripoli, Libya, convicted seventy-five banknote smugglers and sentenced them to death. The defendants were all pigeons.

Hard to believe, but our reps in Congress are comparatively well behaved. Japanese lawmakers commonly engage in fistfights, and British lawmakers loudly heckle the opposition.

The first historical mention of "Blue Laws"—the laws preventing certain activities on Sunday—was found not in official law books, but in a satirical anonymous pamphlet, "The Real Advantages Which Ministers and People May Enjoy, Especially in the Colonies, By Conforming to the Church of England," written in 1762.

In ancient Babylon, you could be killed for giving false testimony.

U.S. courts spend about half of all time on cases directly related to automobiles.

Mobster Al Capone had a brother named Vince. Vince was a police officer.

Dr. Fu Manchu, the fictitious criminal mastermind from books and movies, had medical degrees from three European universities and was an expert in the major languages, chemistry, and botany. If only he'd used his genius for good, instead of evil. . . .

The *J* in J. Edgar Hoover stands for "John." Why he decided to go with Edgar instead is anybody's guess.

Outlaw Clyde Barrow once wrote a fan letter to Henry Ford. "I have drove Fords exclusively when I could get away with one," he scrawled. "Even if my business hasent been strictly legal it don't hurt enything to tell you what a fine car you got in the V-8." He felt that way until the end: a month later he and partner Bonnie Parker were shot dead in a stolen Ford V-8.

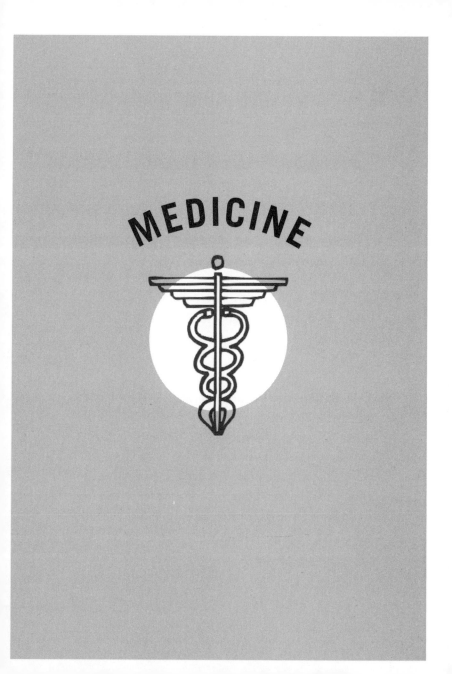

There are about fifteen thousand Americans currently in comas.

The venom from rattlers and other poisonous snakes is used in modern medicines as painkillers, antispasmodics, and blood coagulants.

The cost of prescription drugs is 61 percent lower in Canada than in the United States.

Ancient Egyptian doctors were using penicillin before anyone knew what penicillin was. To treat infections, they placed moldy bread over the wound.

A medical correspondent reminds us to stay away from the barnyard before flu season. Almost all of the flu viruses first infect chickens, then pigs, and then spread to humans, mutating merrily along the way.

Kings like to think they're experts in everything. Henry VIII believed that he'd discovered a cure for syphilis—a paste of powdered pearls and guaiacum resin—which he marketed to his subjects as The King Majesty's Own Plaster.

When anesthesia was first discovered, many fundamentalist Christians opposed its use as being against the will of God. Finally, some bright doctor stilled the controversy by comparing it to the "deep sleep" in which the Bible says God removed one of Adam's ribs in order to make Eve.

The man who invented the birth control pill—Carl Djerassi—also invented an insect repellent based on similar principles: bug hormones that keep creepy crawlers from developing into mature, reproductive adults.

The most ancient form of surgery is trepanning, which means drilling a hole in the skull. Doctors in the Neolithic Age (8000–5500 BC) performed the operation for fractured skulls, convulsions, epilepsy, insanity, and chronic headaches. Interestingly, doctors still use trepanning to relieve pressure in the skull.

Until a hundred years ago, there was no chemical test for diabetes. The only way to check for excessive sugar in the urine was to taste it. A medical book from the 1500s suggested that "it is below the dignity of physicians to do it" and recommended leaving the task to servants or the patients themselves.

It may seem insignificant, but it's been estimated that the common, everyday headache loses businesses $25 billion in productivity every year in the United States.

Ancient Egyptian doctors didn't use anesthesia, but they found an effective alternative—before operating, they whacked the patient on the head with a wooden mallet.

Marijuana mixed with a strong wine   that was the first anesthetic of record, used by Chinese physician Hua T'a while operating in the second century AD.

Forget beige, some researchers have claimed that green in office environments reduce headaches, stomach distress, and other symptoms of stress.

The term "vaccine" comes from the Latin *vacca*, meaning "cows." There's good reason for this. The first successful smallpox vaccine in 1796 was derived from cowpox.

Roll out those lazy, hazy, crazy days of summer: a disproportionate number of people are admitted into mental institutions during the summer months.

Nice guys last and last: according to those bleeding-heart immunologists at Harvard University, practicing humanitarianism helps your immune system fight off illness.

On TV, CPR works most of the time to restart a heart. In real life, alas, it's not that often—only about 15 percent of the people survive.

The "father of comparative anatomy," Aristotle, wasn't a physician at all. He was simply a philosopher who loved to dissect things.

In 1777, most of the world was skeptical about the effectiveness and safety of vaccinations. Still, George Washington had the entire Continental Army vaccinated against smallpox. He had only four thousand men at the time and couldn't afford to lose any to sickness.

There were lots of folks who drank legally during Prohibition in the United States. They just had to get sick to do so. Many medical remedies prescribed by doctors contained alcohol.

Health insurance provider Blue Cross was originally open to schoolteachers only. In 1929, a premium of just $6 per year would cover your hospital fees for up to three weeks.

About twelve thousand U.S. surgeons are qualified to perform transgender operations.

The Quaalude, a hypnotic-sedative drug that became much abused on the black market, was originally created to fight malaria.

Europeans, during the Industrial Revolution, called emphysema and bronchitis "the English disease." Why? Because England had the most cases thanks to "London fog" (air pollution) and a high rate of smoking.

Amynthas of Alexandria performed the first nose job, many believe, sometime in the third century BC.

"Holders down" were medical jobs you probably wouldn't want to apply for. Before anesthesia, hospitals hired burly guys to hold screaming patients securely on the operating table.

Before the 1930s, most emergency ambulance services were provided by funeral homes. Seems to us that it might be a conflict of interest.

In the twelfth century, St. Bernard of Clairvaux, abbot head doctor of the Roman Catholic Church, forbade the monks in his hospitals from studying medical texts and prohibited the use of any remedy but prayer.

Until the 1800s, dental professionals in Europe believed that a type of burrowing worm was what caused tooth decay. The standard treatment was to drop sulfuric acid into the cavity to kill the "worm." All it really did, though, was destroy the nerve tissue.

At least one strain of salmonella is tough enough to survive freezing. Just ask the 224,000 Americans who got sick in 1994 from a salmonella-infested batch of ice cream.

In nineteenth century England, ground-up mummies for mixing into medicines sold for a mere 8 shillings per pound.

Florence Nightingale became famous as a nurse, but she actually served as one for only two years. She contracted a fever while working with patients in the Crimean War and retired, a semi-invalid, for the rest of her life.

The pancreatic tissue of dogs was first used to get insulin for diabetic patients in 1921. After that, medical companies switched to sheep and hogs. Today, most insulin comes from cattle and genetically engineered bacteria.

Dr. Henry Heimlich didn't believe his lifesaving maneuver used on choking people was really that big a deal. He said, "My ultimate goal is to promote well-being for the largest number of people by establishing a philosophy that will eliminate war."

Sigmund Freud was first recognized for his work as a neurologist promoting cocaine as an anaesthetic. Not knowing the addictive perils, his ignorant exuberance for this cure-all drug helped throw Europeans into a wave of cocaine abuse.

The first auto insurance issued was in February of 1898, by Travelers Insurance. It was primarily designed to cover the cost of damage and medical bills in case an auto driver crashed into a horse.

Are you over eighty and male? If so, you have a 90 percent chance of having an enlarged prostate.

Premature babies displayed in incubators were once a very popular staple of Coney Island and World's Fairs. This was before hospitals were willing to invest in the new devices and, to raise funds and public awareness, the inventor decided to appeal directly to the public.

Organ donations suddenly dropped 60 percent in 1978. Nervous transplant surgeons, looking for the reason, noted that the drop coincided with the release of *Coma*, a scary movie about murdering patients for their parts, which was playing to large crowds of potential donors.

Throughout the eighteenth century in Europe, doctors believed that the color red would reduce fever. They'd dress their patients in red nightclothes and surrounded them with red objects.

Jimmy Carter was the first United States president born in a hospital. Before his time, most people were born at home.

To choose the healthiest location for a hospital in ninth-century Baghdad, doctors hung pieces of meat at possible sites. The location where the meat last turned rotten was the one they chose.

Inca surgeons used coca leaves in surgery long before Europeans discovered the anesthetic properties of cocaine. Here's the twist, though—they didn't use it on their patients, they used it on themselves to keep awake and alert during long operations.

Get healthy from smoking? A 1929 Lucky Strikes ad cynically touted "the modern commonsense way—reach for a Lucky instead of a fattening sweet. Everyone is doing it—men keep healthy and fit, women retain a trim figure."

MEN and WOMEN

Listen up, civil engineers: Women take nearly twice as long to use the restroom than men—a whopping thirty-four seconds longer. Women should, therefore, have nearly twice as many facilities.

From the Romance files: Thomas Edison and his wife Mina used to talk to each other privately at parties by tapping out messages in Morse code into each other's hands. In fact, that's how he proposed to her.

Believe it or not, comedians have a lower divorce rate than any other showbiz group.

Patriot Patrick Henry, the "give me liberty or give me death" guy, left his estate to his wife as long as she didn't take the liberty of remarrying after his death. "It would make me unhappy to feel I have worked all my life to support another man's wife." She ditched the money for love and remarried.

In contrast, poet Heinrich Heine stipulated that his widow must remarry before inheriting his estate, "so at least one other man will regret my death."

Eleanor Roosevelt's maiden name was Eleanor Roosevelt. She was a distant cousin of Franklin's; when she married him, she didn't have to update her driver's license or stationary.

Anthropologists believe that it was only about eight thousand years ago that humans realized that men had anything to do with starting pregnancies.

Something to think about when pondering medicine and romance: women reject heart transplants more often than men.

In 1893, New Zealand became the first country to allow women to vote in national elections. Ninety thousand women showed up for the big event that year.

Gaydar, the unspoken cues between gay men, isn't a recent invention. When Oscar Wilde met Walt Whitman, the much older Whitman looked Wilde in the eye and then, before saying anything, kissed him squarely on the lips.

Write what you know, say the writing teachers. Norman Mailer's *An American Dream* is about a guy who stabs his wife. It was based on Mailer's real-life experience of the time he stabbed his own wife.

Ski instructors say that men tend to fall on their faces, women on their rears, because his center of gravity is usually higher than hers.

More boys are born during the day than girls; more girls are born at night than boys.

PLANTS

The stink of onion was once thought strong enough to scare off illness. Oniony folk remedies have included onion tea to stop a fever, rubbing an onion on your head if you have a headache, and smearing turpentine with fried onions on your chest to choke out a cold. (Perhaps the fear of having to repeat the prescription was enough to cure the illness.)

Watch out for cherry trees. Even though the fruit is divine, eating the leaves and limbs can be fatal.

More than half of the peanuts grown in the United States are made into peanut butter. About a quarter are sold as roasted peanuts, and most of the rest are made into peanut oil.

Cashews are closely related to poison ivy. So are the mango and the ginkgo tree.

A single coffee tree yields only about 2–4 pounds of roasted coffee annually.

Hydrogen cyanide. That's the poisonous gas that is released when you digest pits from peaches, cherries, plums, apricots, or apples. In enough quantity, it can kill you.

Poisonous mushrooms? Squirrels don't pay them no never mind. They eat mushrooms that would kill a human and scamper away with no bad result whatsoever.

The toadstool mushroom's name comes from the German *todesstuhl*, meaning "death's stool." The name was garbled in translation to English.

A simple, everyday yard mushroom can release more than one hundred million spores in an hour.

One good sugar maple will give you about 35 gallons of sap. Boiled down and bottled, that equals about a gallon of syrup.

Thinking of a living holiday tree for environmental reasons? Holiday lights on potted pine trees doesn't hurt them. What does hurt them is being brought from the outside into warm, dry air for a while and then put outside again. The change in environment is too stressful for many trees to handle.

Cowslips are called that because they're especially adept at growing in the *meadow muffins* that cows leave behind.

Smut is a mold that grows in corn ears and looks like dirt. Once people started thinking of sexual content as dirty, it was just a matter of time before the word spread from corn to porn.

If you're starving in the woods, you can safely eat the inner layers of pine bark. Not that it's tasty, mind you, but it will fend off starvation.

What do you do if you're trying to market a healthy food product with a horrible name? Trademark a more euphonious name and make money licensing it to growers. That's essentially the story of how oil from the rape plant, a member of the mustard family, is now marketed as "canola oil."

It's illegal to own gerbils in California. The fear is that the little varmints will get loose and multiply, devastating the state's crops.

Not just for tofu any more: soybeans go into the making of many products including cosmetics, linoleum, paint, inks, diesel fuel, biodegradable plastics, and even parts in your car.

All evidence suggests that a mastodon's favorite food was the water lily. Specimens of the mastodon have been found with the partially digested stalks and leaves in their stomachs.

A pimpernel is a flower—one that closes as bad weather approaches. For this reason, it's sometimes called "the poor man's weather glass." Pimpernels come in a variety of colors, including scarlet.

George Washington Carver formulated more than 325 products made from peanuts. He also found 75 different things to make with pecans, 108 products made from sweet potatoes, and more than 500 natural dyes from plants.

It can take twelve to forty-eight hours for a poison ivy rash to appear after you've come into contact with the plant oils, and it can linger for up to ten miserably itchy days.

No surprise to chocolate lovers, cocoa seeds were a form of currency in pre-Columbian America. A rabbit cost eight seeds for the average Mayan; a slave cost one hundred.

Theobroma cacao, the fruit with a seed that produces chocolate, translates from Greek as "food of the gods."

RELIGION, HOLIDAYS, and TRADITIONS

Who came up with the idea of a holiday to honor working people? During America's Gilded Age, as the rich became increasingly rich and insular, machinist Matthew Maguire and carpenter Peter J. McGuire organized a march in New York City in September 1882 in which tens of thousands of workers took an unpaid day off in support of organizing labor.

Workers definitely needed something. According to the 1890 census, eleven million of the nation's twelve million families earned less than $1,200 per year (the equivalent of $22,700 today). Of this group, the average annual family income was well below the poverty line at $380 ($7,200 today).

In China, a country full of both divination and tea, reading tea leaves is all but unknown.

Sure Halloween, Valentine's Day, and Christmas are big, but Easter is the holiday season when Americans buy the most candy of all.

Vlad the Impaler—the inspiration for the fictional character Dracula—studied to be a priest before becoming a tyrant and sadist.

Americans send over three billion Christmas cards each year.

What does a *K* or a *U* on a food product mean? That it has been pronounced kosher by a rabbi.

In 1401, the English Parliament decreed that citizens who were caught with an English-language Bible were to be burned alive.

Wedding cake was originally provided as something to throw at the new bride and groom. Unfrosted, luckily.

In Europe, taking baths fell out of favor for twelve centuries after the Catholic church decreed in 500 AD that exposing your skin—even to yourself—was a sin.

"What would Jesus do" with the information that there are more than twelve hundred different Christian denominations in the United States and Canada?

As a sign of mourning over a dead king or captain, a ship's riggings were allowed to hang in limp disarray. From this came the practice on land and sea of lowering the flag to half mast.

For humanitarian reasons, the Vatican in 1139 outlawed the use of crossbows in war . . . unless they were being used against Muslims.

Originally Groundhog's Day was called Candlemas, and the animal used to predict the onset of spring wasn't a groundhog at all, but a badger. Unfortunately, there were no badgers in the New World, so German immigrants had to substitute a different ground-dwelling mammal.

Want an easy Bible verse to memorize for Sunday School? Choose the shortest verse in the whole book: "Jesus wept." (John 11:35)

Looking for that boringly traditional Father's Day present? Keep in mind that the bestselling tie colors are blue, followed by red.

Only eighty-five million Father's Day cards are sent each year, as opposed to 150 million on Mother's Day.

More calls are made in the United States on Mother's Day than any other day. More collect phone calls are made in the United States on Father's Day.

For whatever reason, people steer clear of funny cards for Mother's Day, but love them for Father's Day.

A religious reader writes to remind us that it was a French monk—Dom Perignon—who invented champagne.

"Seeing-eye dogs" got their name from Proverbs 20:12 "The seeing eye, the hearing ear; the Lord hath made them both."

The slow pace of a funeral procession may have come from the use of candelabras in the procession. If the pace were any faster, the candles would go out. The candelabras were called "herses." With time, an *a* was added and the word extended to include the cart that carried both the candles and the deceased.

Halloween traditions began perhaps 2800 years ago as a celebration of the Celtic lord of death, Samhain. Celts believed that Samhain allowed the souls of the dead to return to earth on October 31.

In the ninth century AD, the Catholic church established All Saints' Day on November 1 to compete with the Samhain festival. The church service was called "Allhallowmas," so the ghostly night before became known as "Allhallow e'en."

Trick-or-treating likely came from the ninth century custom of souling. Christian beggars would go door to door, promising to pray for your dead relatives if you'd give them a current-filled "soul cake" baked for the occasion.

Halloween pranks in your great-great-great-grandfather's day included taking the hinges off the neighbors' gate and tipping over their outhouse.

In 1871, a Pennsylvania man sued Satan and his minions for putting obstacles in his path and causing his downfall. The case was thrown out of court on the grounds that the defendant did not reside in the state.

Thinking in advance about this year's Christmas cards? You can get them sent with a decorative postmark from Santa Claus, Indiana by sending them pre-stamped in a large envelope to: Postmaster, Santa Claus Station, Santa Claus, IN 47579-9998.

Every book of the standard Bible mentions wine, except for Jonah. The book of Isaiah even has advice on how to plant a good vineyard.

As a young man, Abraham Lincoln wrote a pamphlet that argued against the divinity of Jesus and against the divine inspiration of the Bible. He ultimately heeded his friends' advice not to publish it because it would likely wreck his political career.

More Californians believe they've been abducted by aliens than residents in any other state. Surprised? Neither are we.

SCIENCE and TECHNOLOGY

In September of 1888, George Eastman patented his roll film camera and registered the name Kodak—coined, he said, because he wanted a distinctive name and really liked the letter *K*.

Douglas Engelbart originally created the X-Y Position Indicator for a Display System in the late 1960s. "XYPIDS" didn't catch on as a name for the invention. Early users called them "turtles" instead. Eventually users adopted "rodent," which became the cuter-sounding "mouse," the name that finally stuck to that computer device that rolls and clicks.

How did weirdly secretive Howard Hughes amass his fortune? He was born rich, thanks to his father who invented a drill bit used by oil explorers.

Alexander Graham Bell insisted that "Hoy! Hoy!" was the only proper way to answer a ringing telephone. It was his friend Thomas Edison who popularized "hello" instead.

If you don't have a tuning fork, pick up the phone. The higher note of the dial tone is 440 cycles per second, which is a perfect A.

If you counted out one trillion seconds, it would take you more than 31,688 years.

In the United States, a billion means 1,000,000,000. In England, it means 1,000,000,000,000.

Foiled again! Richard Reynolds invented metal foil wrap, but not for food. It was at the behest of his uncle and cigarette magnate R.J. Reynolds, to keep tobacco fresh.

Thomas Edison didn't want his phonograph sold for amusement purposes: "It's not a toy. It is for business purposes only."

Want somebody to blame for being woken up so early this morning? Try Levi Hutchins of Concord, New Hampshire. He's the guy who in 1787 invented the alarm clock.

Window glass is made perfectly smooth on both sides by floating molten glass on top of molten tin. Since the melting point of tin is lower, the glass cools enough to become solid.

Thank Walter Alcock of England next time you're in the bathroom. He's the man who invented toilet paper as we know it (perforated and on a roll). That was in 1879.

The French Revolution brought us the metric system. Since they were changing everything else, thought the new government, why not also come up with a logical way of measuring?

The revolutionary French government introduced a metric clock with ten hours in a day, each consisting of one hundred minutes of one hundred seconds each. The week went ten days, the last of which was a day of rest. However, workers accustomed to having every seventh day off screamed that they were being robbed, and the system collapsed.

The Hope Diamond was once part of France's crown jewels. During the revolution the jewels were looted and the humongous diamond disappeared. When it reappeared twenty years later, its 67 carats had been cut down to 45, presumably to disguise its origins.

Dr. Ivan Pavlov won the Nobel Prize in 1904, but it was not because of his now-famous bell and slobbering dogs. Instead, it was because of his work on the automatic nervous system—which time subsequently proved to be scientifically insignificant.

In 1800, nitrous oxide was solely used for entertainment purposes. "Laughing gas" parties became intoxicating pastimes. By 1844, though, a Connecticut dentist named Horace Wells tried some on himself and found he could extract a tooth painlessly.

Dr. Lillian Moller Gilbreth invented the electric food mixer and the foot-pedal trashcan. You may know her as "Mother" from the book her children wrote, *Cheaper by the Dozen*.

There was a time when Japanese laws regulated the colors of their office equipment. It's the main reason why Jerry Manock—designer of the Apple II—made the new computer beige, which pretty much stuck until those flamboyantly colored iMacs came along.

Rumors that the Great Wall can be seen from the moon are more loony than lunar, according to eyewitness accounts by astronauts. They swear that it is absolutely not true.

One chest x-ray gives you about the same amount of radiation as the normal background radiation you receive from the sun over three days.

The concept of the endothermic reaction (the principle at work in modern ice packs) is nothing new. By the 1550s, Italians were using a mix of saltpeter and water to cool their liquor bottles.

If the Earth were a ball with a diameter of four feet, our atmosphere would be only $\frac{1}{25}$ inch thick.

Little Brother is watching you. According to a company that installs security cameras, a person spending an average day in New York City will be videotaped about seventy-four times.

If you're looking at career possibilities, best cross bank robber off your list. What with surveillance equipment, bulletproof teller stations, exploding money packs, and quick-responding cops, 70 percent of all robbers get caught. Even if you escape, the average successful robbery yields less than $6,500. Hardly worth the trouble.

Microwaves are just very short radio waves. If you could turn your radio dial to 2500 megahertz, you could hear your microwave oven broadcasting. (Alas, most radio dials only go as high as 108 megahertz.)

In the 1930s, Antabuse, a drug used for alcoholism, was discovered by accident in a rubber manufacturing plant. Workers who worked with tetraethylthiuram disulfide discovered that they became violently ill if they drank alcohol. The therapeutic use of the chemical soon followed.

Temperatures on the moon fluctuate from 273° F during the day to minus 243° F at night. Astronauts can withstand the higher temps in their suits, but the lower ones are just too cold, which is why landings are timed for daytime.

Thomas Jefferson wasn't just a founding father, but an inventor, too. His inventions included a plow designed for turning dirt on hills, a cipher wheel for sending coded messages (his principle was later used in kids' "decoder rings"), a copying contraption he called the polygraph, and a swivel chair.

How's this for a life? Samuel Breese Morse, artist and sculptor, helped found New York City's National Academy of Design in 1826. Eleven years later, he patented the telegraph. Later he entered politics as an anti-abolishionist, believing that slavery had been ordained by the Bible.

When the electric toothbrush was invented, it was first tested on dogs. They reportedly enjoyed the sensation, and the brush went on to big commercial success with humans, too.

The Wright brothers were ahead of their time: they built a rudimentary wind tunnel and tested their flight designs first with model airplanes before constructing their full-size planes.

Parachutes were originally invented to save the lives of passengers in hot air balloons. The first demonstration came in 1797 when a Frenchman named André Garnerin strapped on a parachute and deliberately jumped from a balloon. To the amazement of the crowds below, he survived.

Have you heard a tornado described as an "F-3"? The *F* stands for "Fujita"—Dr. Tetsuya Fujita, the man responsible for thinking up the measuring system.

If you've gotten close enough to care, a skunk's stench comes from a combination of six different sulfur compounds. Why doesn't washing work? Because only three of the sulfur compounds activate at first spray; the other three begin stinking when they're mixed with water.

The first wireless radio message transmitted was the Morse code for *S*. It was 1901 and Italian physicist Guglielmo Marconi—whether he knew it or not—had just given birth to radio.

Anyone remember the Rejuvinator? It was a 1920s candy bar that was laced with a weak dose of radium. At the time, people believed that the dangerous element would make you strong.

Before they became musical genres, "acid rock," "hard rock," and "country rock" were geological terms. "Heavy metal," however, came from the field of chemistry.

Since 1790, the U.S. Patent Office has issued more than five million patents.

It's not true that you can't tour the Nevada Test Site where nuclear bombs were tried out during the Cold War. You can reserve a spot for one of the monthly tours, but enter at your own risk. One of the highlights, says the Department of Energy Web site, is a nuclear bomb crater 1,280 feet in diameter and 320 feet deep.

Cirrus clouds are the high, wispy, spidery ones. In Latin cirrus means "tendril."

Rain-resistant fabric Gore-Tex was originally created as coating for electrical wires.

How the Shakers were able to make great furniture: Tabitha Babbit, a sister at a Shaker colony, adapted a foot-driven spinning wheel and invented the circular saw in 1813.

In 1945, when scientists at the Manhattan Project set off the first atomic bomb in Alamogordo, New Mexico, physicist Enrico Fermi set up a $1 betting pool about how big the explosion would be. Bets ranged from predictions the bomb would be a dud to one man who betted that it would destroy the entire world.

An airplane's "black box" isn't black. It's fluorescent orange with white stripes to make it easier to see. Most people don't know that the black box isn't in the cockpit—it's mounted in the back of the plane, which is more likely to stay intact if the plane crashes.

St. Isadora of Seville is the patron saint of computer programmers and the Internet.

Kids, don't try this at home. In 1944, Flight Sergeant Nicholas Alkemade jumped from his flaming British Lancaster bomber and fell 17,000 feet without a parachute. Miraculously, he bounced off a fir tree, landed in a snow bank, and survived without even breaking a bone.

How fast is that roller coaster? Not as fast as it seems. Disney's Space Mountain, for example, never goes faster than 37 mph.

SPORTS

Tug of War was an Olympic event from 1900 to 1920. Since even badminton qualifies these days, we'd like to know why they haven't revived this playground standard, too.

Tiger Woods got his first hole in one at age six.

Shoeless Joe Jackson still hasn't made it into baseball's Hall of Fame. However, his shoes are on display there.

Something to keep in mind as the storm clouds approach: 12 percent of all lightning fatalities in America happen on a golf course.

Dodging trolley cars was what most Brooklyn pedestrians had to do a lot of in the early 1900s. That's how the Brooklyn baseball team became known as the Trolley Dodgers, and then just the Dodgers.

It was traditional for ancient Greek Olympic athletes to compete in the buff. Women weren't invited.

They'd better do some studying between games: Only 8 percent of college baseball, basketball, and football players even make the draft for their pro sport. Only 2 percent make it onto a professional team.

The father of professional golfer Lee Trevino was a gravedigger.

Englanders in the 1700s enjoyed brutal "sports" like bull running, which consisted of a mob of people running down a bull and killing it. England finally banned many of the blood sports in 1835.

Hundreds of years ago, German monks believed that if a man was a good bowler, it was a sign that he was a godly man.

Based on ticket sales and attendance records, the most popular sport in the world is horse racing.

In 1921, as Babe Ruth became tremendously famous for his ball playing, a city slicker named Otto Schnering rushed out the Baby Ruth candy bar. When challenged by the ballplayer's lawyers, Schnering disingenuously claimed that he'd named the bar after former president Grover Cleveland's preteen daughter who had died of diphtheria seventeen years earlier. To add injury to insult, Schnering then successfully blocked Ruth from using his own name on the Babe Ruth Home Run Bar.

Thinking of golfing in Australia? Golfers there warn that crows and currawongs swoop down and steal balls. When one bird's nest was blasted with a water cannon, nearly fifty balls came raining down.

Traditionally, polo balls were carved out of willow root. However, hard plastic has been making inroads into the sport. Bucky, Biff, and Poppy are very likely appalled.

The highest scoring professional baseball game? After an excruciatingly long game on a hot August day in 1922, the Chicago Cubs edged out the Philadelphia Phillies, 26 to 23.

At the Talamore Golf Course in Southern Pines, North Carolina, you have the option of renting either a golf cart or a llama to carry your bags.

Bat Masterson made a smooth transition from Wild West gunfighter to life in the modern world: he became a sports writer for the *New York Morning Telegraph*. After two decades of word-slingin', he died with his boots on, in front of his typewriter at work.

Most circus performances look dangerous (and would be for the average Joe). But it's a fact that spectators suffer more injuries and death traveling to and from the circus than do performers in their acts.

It's specifically against the rules for left-handers to play jai alai. Well, that's not completely true. Left-handers can play—as long as they use their right hands.

There aren't many atheists in a sand bunker. One survey found that nearly 75 percent of golfers said that they've prayed while playing the game.

We love this one from Babe Didrikson, athlete extraordinaire: "It's not enough just to swing at the ball; you've got to loosen your girdle and really let the ball have it."

There are typically between 360 and 523 dimples on a golf ball. Each measures up to .01 of an inch deep.

Baseball cards were originally packaged, not with bubblegum, but with cigarettes. Back in 1887, you could get a card in your pack of Dog's Head, Old Judge, or Gypsy Queen smokes.

Despite its Canadian roots, the first professional hockey league originated in the United States.

Mush! A good dog sled team can get you moving at about 20 mph over snow and ice.

How many Supreme Court justices played professional football? As far as we know, only one. Byron "Whizzer" White, the NFL's top rusher in 1938. He played for the Pittsburgh Pirates (now known as the Steelers) for three years before entering law.

Before the first portable golf tees were invented in the late 1800s, golfers pushed up a pile of sand to tee off.

When Muhammad Ali was a child, he had his brother throw rocks at him to practice his dodging skills. Although his brother thought he was nuts, he never passed up the opportunity to try. He also never hit him.

The Wilson Sporting Goods Company was a spin-off of a meatpacking firm. In 1913, it was looking for a way to dispose of the leftover animals parts that kept piling up at the slaughterhouse. Wilson's first products included baseball shoes, sutures, and two types of tennis racquets.

The first permanent golfing club in the Western hemisphere was the Royal Montreal Golf Club, established in 1873.

The first U.S. president to golf was William McKinley.

The speed of a typical golfer's swing is 101 mph.

Ever wonder who started golf's Ryder Cup? It was Samuel Ryder, a wealthy Englishman who made his fortune selling penny packets of flower seeds. His original prize in 1926: a champagne and chicken sandwich dinner for all competitors and $5 for the winner.

In 1960, Green Bay Packer Paul Hornung scored the most points ever—176—in one pro season. He was not only their star halfback, but the guy who kicked field goals for extra points as well.

In 1899, a Yale divinity student named Amos Alonzo Stagg invented the tackling dummy.

Before Johannes Gutenberg started publishing Bibles on his printing press invention, he was turning out playing cards for gamblers.

According to a study, about 80 percent of the six million pathological gamblers are men. Three-quarters of them brag about winning even when they're losing.

The longest single hole on a golf course is the sixth at the Koolan Island course in Australia. It measures 948 yards and is a par 7 hole.

Basketball, volleyball, and rodeo are three sports invented in the United States. No, baseball wasn't. Neither was football.

Why are golfers called duffers? It was commentary. The Scottish word "duffar," or "doofart," meant "a dull or stupid person."

"Hooker in the Scrum" is not an unpublished novel by J.D. Salinger, but a method in rugby for deciding control of the play. Forwards of both rugby teams form a circle and then see which side can maneuver the ball out of the circle first.

Despite what you might've seen in the movie, *A League of Their Own*, a baseball player can't legally catch a ball in her cap. It has to be by glove or hand, nothing else.

Ever wonder why tennis balls are so fuzzy? It's mostly to slow the game down. The fuzz makes the ball less bouncy. It also increases wind resistance. A side benefit is that the fuzz grips the strings of the racquet slightly, allowing more spin and ball control.

Which sports event lasts about two minutes, but is watched by millions each year? No, not the Super Bowl with commercials removed—it's the Kentucky Derby.

Unlike wrestling, there are no weight classes in the sport of sumo wrestling. A lightweight *sumotori* has to rely on reaction time, skill, and speed to bring down a much heavier opponent.

Famous Olympians include General George Patton (1912, pentathlon; no medal), baby doctor Benjamin Spock (1924, rowing; no medal), England's Princess Anne (1976, horses; no medal), and Erector Set inventor Alfred C. Gilbert (1908, pole vault; gold medal).

"Beware before!" That's what men of the British artillery shouted at the infantry before shooting over their heads. In battle, that was a little wordy, so it became shortened to "Fore!" Sometime around 1770, golfers adopted the custom of shouting the same thing when driving.

The Dutch game of *kolven*—played on any hard surface—has the distinction of being the first golf-like game European colonists played in the New World. It was also the first to be banned. A 1659 ordinance of Fort Orange, New York, forbids "all persons from playing *het kolven* in the streets."

Jai alai players need a wicker basket on a stick, a rubber and goatskin ball, and extremely fast reflexes. The ball careens at speeds of up to 188 mph and has been known to kill a player now and again.

Jai alai, by the way, means "merry festival" in the Basque language.

Albert Doubleday didn't invent baseball in Cooperstown, as legend has it. It evolved from the English games of cricket and rounders, which was known as "base ball" long before Doubleday was born.

Take a cue from John Hyatts. He was the guy who patented the billiard ball in 1865.

The first televised sport was a baseball game between Awazi Shichiku and Ushigome elementary schools in Japan. The year was 1931.

In 2004, the Baseball Hall of Fame finally exhibited Shoeless Joe Jackson's uniform, glove, and other baseball momentos next to his shoes, which were already on display.

Jack Norworth and Albert von Tilzer wrote the classic song, "Take Me Out to the Ballgame." Neither had ever seen a game in 1908 when they wrote it, they just knew baseball was a new novelty that might sell a few songs.

Billy Ripken's 1989 Fleer card held a little surprise for baseball card collectors. Someone had strategically written an obscenity on the bottom of his bat that features quite prominently in the shot. Fleer eventually corrected the gaffe, but there are still quite a few of these out there.

The notorious briefcase with nuclear weapon codes that the U.S. president has near him at all times is casually referred to in presidential circles as "the football."

Baseball trading cards were once the prize in boxes of Cracker Jacks.

From 1961 to 1963, Post issued baseball cards on the back of their cereal boxes.

You think a hole in one's an impossible dream? Not according to a golfer named Scott Palmer. Between June 1983 and June 1984, Palmer made thirty-three of those aces on the golf course.

In the 1890s, the Pittsburgh Alleghenies, a baseball team named for the nearby Allegheny River, managed to steal away some players from a rival club. Thereafter, they were known as the Pittsburgh Pirates.

 The torch and five-ring logo in the Olympics didn't come from the ancient Greeks. It first appeared in the 1936 Berlin Olympic games, which were hosted by the pageant-loving Nazis.

Nowadays, an Olympic torch is 32 inches of wood, aluminum, and gold-plated brass. It weighs about 3½ pounds. A small tank in the base holds about forty minutes worth of propane. They cost about $300 to make. About ten thousand are made for each Olympics so that runners in the intercontinental relay can keep the one they ran with.

There are still two golf balls on the moon. Both were hit by astronaut Alan Shepard, who didn't play them were they lay and didn't have a caddy to retrieve them.

Early names for bat and ball games from the nineteenth century include "rounders," "town ball," and "one old cat."

Sumo wrestling began as a religious event and is still full of symbolic ritual. In fact, the ceremony before a sumo wrestling match lasts much longer than the match itself.

Count the Cincinnati Reds as minor victims of 1950s McCarthyism. Not wanting to have to defend their team name to the House of Un-American Activities Committee, the team quietly changed its name to the Redlegs for a few years.

Keep it straight: a scrimmage is from American football, but scrummage is from rugby.

Sumo wrestlers have it easy nowadays. Two thousand years ago, the losers were often killed.

Say you're playing golf in a hurricane or an earthquake. If you've begun your swing but your ball falls off the tee before you can hit it, it still counts as a stroke.

Football was nearly outlawed in the United States in 1909. In that year, twenty-seven players died and hundreds more were permanently injured. A blue-ribbon committee headed by Princeton University president Woodrow Wilson changed the rules, banning things like diving tackles, blocking with linked arms, and picking up and carrying the guy with the ball, all of which drastically cut the number of deaths and injuries.

You're twelve times more likely to get injured playing football than baseball.

Two-thirds of all basketball injuries are knee related. Blame all those sudden stops and starts in high-friction shoes.

The worst shutout in football history took place in 1916, when Georgia Tech squeaked past Cumberland University 222 to 0.

These guys are too good! In the 1956 Tasmanian Golf Open, the winner was Peter Toogood. His dad, Alfred Toogood, came in second, and his brother, John Toogood, came in third.

In 1897, Louis Sockalexis was the first known Native American to play major league baseball. His presence on the roster of the Cleveland Spiders spawned the team's better-known name: spectators mockingly called them the Cleveland Indians.

It was the football team of Canada's McGill University that first introduced the egg-shaped ball to American football.

Carl Stotz founded Little League baseball in 1939. However, he became so disgusted with the behavior of parents and coaches that he disavowed the organization in 1955.

TRANSPORTATION

Henry Ford's first car was called the Quadricycle Runabout.

Would you buy a car called the Pastelogram, Piluma, Mongoose Cigique, or Utopian Turtletop? All of these names were considered for a futuristic car model in the late 1950s, but the company decided to play it safe and name the car after the company founder's late son. It didn't help—the funny-looking Ford Edsel became a marketing laughingstock.

July, for some reason, is the most dangerous month for fatal car accidents. February's next.

The record speed for a unicycle from a standing start is 18.5 mph.

Why did railways of old insist that patrons not use the restrooms while the train was in the station? Because the trains didn't have holding tanks—the "toilets" were simply holes in the bottom of the car that let waste dump directly onto the ground.

More people are injured each year on merry-go-rounds than on roller coasters.

The U.S. organization with the most members is the American Automobile Association, or AAA.

While the Wright brothers can lay claim to the very first successful airplane flight, they can also claim the first fatal airplane crash. A passenger on one of their early flights was killed on impact. This was before seatbelts, floating seat cushions, or even seats.

J.R.R. Tolkien, *Lord of the Rings* author and scholar at Oxford, never owned a car.

Not everyone hates billboards. In 1959, McDonald's spokeswoman June Martino argued that restricting them would be detrimental to travelers: "Uninterrupted scenery can get pretty monotonous. Billboards are only a way of humanizing what is still an overwhelming landscape."

The ships that were boarded by revolutionaries for the Boston Tea Party were named the *Eleanor*, the *Beaver*, and the *Dartmouth*.

It was 1901 when the first state—New York—required all motor vehicles be licensed.

This will come as no surprise to those with navy experience, but the German U-boat gets its name from the German *unterseeboot*. Considering that the U-boat is a submarine, this name makes sense. It means "under sea boat."

It's a point of record that Charles Lindbergh, for good luck and comfort, took a Felix the Cat doll with him on his famous transatlantic flight.

History repeats itself: the absurdly oversized autos of the 1950s lowered average gas mileage from 20 miles per gallon to 12.

When asked by a Los Angeles County supervisor to increase gas mileage, decrease pollution, and add safety features, a 1950s auto executive responded: "Will this sell more cars? Will it look prettier? Will it give us more horsepower? If not, we're not interested."

There are nearly four million miles of paved roads in the United States; in 1900, there were only 150 miles.

Train whistles carry specific messages. For instance, one toot means that the train's approaching a station.

Two long toots, one short toot, and one long toot mean that the train's coming to a crossing. Three short blasts means the train's backing up. And short repeated toots means "Get off the track, you idiot!"

One of Walt Disney's favorite pastimes was painstakingly planning train wrecks on his half a mile of miniature train tracks.

On its pilgrim-laden voyage across the Atlantic, the *Mayflower* took sixty-five days, averaging a speed of 2 mph. Its return trip, traveling with prevailing winds, took only thirty-one days.

Not only is the London Underground the world's longest subway with 244 miles of track; it's also the world's oldest. It opened in 1863.

To save weight, Charles Lindbergh carried a bare minimum on his famous nonstop trip across the Atlantic. He had no navigational equipment or radio. When he saw a fishing fleet below, he moved in close, cut his engines, and bellowed, "Which way to Ireland?"

In 1900, electric automobiles accounted for 38 percent of all U.S. car sales. Unfortunately, the cars' speeds were limited to about 20 mph and they had to be recharged every fifty miles, so their popularity dwindled.

Where will it end? In 1890, there were only about one hundred registered motor vehicles in the United States. By 1900, we were up to eight thousand cars and, by 1915, 2,491,000. Today, we've got 160 million.

"Motown" comes from "Motor Town," a nickname for car-heavy Detroit, Michigan.

Inmates in New Hampshire produce license plates. This isn't really unusual, but here's the irony—stamped on each plate is the state's motto: Live Free or Die.

According to research, the most visible (and therefore safest) colors for your car are bright blue and yellow. White's not bad either, unless you drive in snow. But if you drive a gray or dark green car, keep your headlights on. The eye has the hardest time seeing these colors in almost any light.

If you poll the folks in Gallup, New Mexico, you'll find that they're downright proud that there are twice as many pickup trucks in their city than cars.

By the 1920s, Henry Ford was already recycling leftover metal from his production line, but he was disturbed by how much wood was thrown out. Ford convinced Edward Kingsford, his cousin's husband, to recycle the wood scraps into charcoal briquettes. The Kingsford Company still makes charcoal today.

Ever wonder where the phrase "pushing the envelope" came from? It was coined by test pilots in the 1940s. The range of performance that was safe for a particular aircraft was known as its "envelope," so "pushing it" meant testing beyond the specs, risking disaster. The phrase was introduced into mainstream language by the movie, *The Right Stuff.*

The first known airplane-related crime took place on November 12, 1926. Gangsters buzzed the farmhouse hideaway of a rival gang in Williamson County, Illinois, and dropped three small bombs. None of the bombs exploded, and nobody was hurt.

Do you want to know which direction a train route will take you? In most cases, even-numbered trains travel north and east. Odd-numbered trains travel south and west.

ABOUT THE AUTHORS

Erin Barrett and Jack Mingo have authored twenty-one books, including *Ben Franklin's Guide to Wealth, It Takes a Certain Type to Be a Writer, The Couch Potato Guide to Life,* and the best-selling *Just Curious Jeeves.* They have written articles for many major periodicals including *The New York Times, Salon, Reader's Digest,* and *The Washington Post* and have generated more than thirty thousand questions for trivia games and game shows.

Their column appears in the Minneapolis *Star-Tribune,* the *Contra Costa Times,* and many other papers. Erin and Jack live in the San Francisco Bay area and welcome questions at *ask@mingo-barrett.com.*